A HOLINESS OF THE HEART

THE
METHODIST
CENTRE

19 STRATFORD ROAD
BROMSGROVE
WORCS. B60 1AS

THERE IS <u>POWER</u>
IN THE <u>BLOOD</u>
OF <u>JESUS CHRIST</u>

A Holiness of the Heart

DAVID WILKINSON

MONARCH
BOOKS

First published by Monarch Books in 2000

ISBN 1 85424 457 4

British Library Cataloguing Data
A catalogue record for this book is available
from the British Library.

Designed and produced for the publishers by
Bookprint Creative Services
P.O. Box 827, BN21 3YJ, England
Printed in Great Britain.

To Elm Hall Drive Methodist Church
and the student Methodist Society
for teaching me so much about Jesus

CONTENTS

ACKNOWLEDGEMENTS

This is a book which comes out of local church life. For the past eight years I have been one of the ministers at Elm Hall Drive Methodist Church and one of the chaplains at Liverpool University and Liverpool Hope University College. All the following chapters started life as sermons preached either in our morning all-age worship, the traditional evening service or the contemporary eight o'clock service. As sermons they have been both created and refined with many people. They are a testimony to the way that my life has been enriched by the love and support of the people and students of Liverpool, especially those who are a part of the church I have been privileged to serve.

It has also been a privilege to see God transform the lives of individuals and some of those stories are recounted in this book. The stories are not just from Liverpool but refer to ministry in other parts of the country. In stories about certain individuals, names, sexes and places have been changed to respect their privacy.

The writing of this book has also been made possible by the Circuit and Church encouraging me to take a three-month sabbatical. In particular I would like to thank my present colleagues Karen George, Jonathan Budd, Myf Threlfall and the

Rev. Ann Le Mare, who carried a great deal more work during the sabbatical. The superintendent of the Circuit, the Rev. Carl Howarth, the Circuit stewards and the church stewards of Elm Hall Drive all made the sabbatical possible. My support group once again were a constant source of encouragement and help.

Lucy Brooke, James Cook, Vicky Moverley and Alison Wilkinson made helpful suggestions and did work on the manuscript. Tony Collins was as good a publisher as ever. Adam and Hannah Wilkinson were a creative distraction from the task of writing and continue to teach Daddy about priorities. None of my writing is possible without the encouragement and theological wisdom of my wife Alison, who shares with me our thankfulness for the Christian community here in Liverpool which has given us so much.

INTRODUCTION

It's amazing how quickly things come in and out of fashion. A few days ago, I saw the most amazing sight. Four professional women were teaching a dance to the song 'Tragedy' by the British group Steps, to my five-year-old son and two-year-old daughter. The museum curator, the staff nurse, the graphic designer and the trainee teacher were enjoying it as much as the children!

My tragedy is that I remember the song the first time round when the Bee Gees sang it. At that stage the Bee Gees were becoming a little uncool and so I admitted to very few that I rather liked the song. However, a decade later, the Bee Gees have become cool again, appearing at the Brit awards and having their songs covered by all the new bands. However, I suspect for all of their talent, there will come a day when Steps will be uncool and my grown-up son will cringe to know that his father ever wrote these paragraphs.

From music to fashion, from personalities to philosophies, we live in an ever-changing world. The Church is not immune to such changes. Working with students over the past eight years has shown me clearly some of these changes. Particular churches in the city, including our own, go in and out of fashion as the place to go. In terms of music, not only are hymns condemned as out of date, but to some in our church unless the song is written by Martin Smith or Matt Redman then it's simply 'old and boring'. Speakers and conferences gain in popularity until a point is reached where they lose their appeal.

I sympathise with much of this, for it is a reflection of the world we live in. However, leaving aside churches, music or personalities, I believe that it is a tragedy when particular biblical truth is cast aside or ignored. In this generation I believe that this has happened to the biblical doctrine of holiness – and I feel passionately about it.

'Holiness' is not very popular today. Advertise a talk on 'A Christian view of sex' or 'Healing in the power of the Spirit' and you can guarantee an excited, packed congregation. A talk on 'holiness' may receive the same enthusiasm as 'Advanced tax returns – for very sad people'. When Hodder and Stoughton brought out a new edition of the Bible they simply called it 'The Bible'. A spokesperson said, 'We dropped the word "Holy" to give it a more mass market appeal.'

I am always amazed when I go to my local Christian bookshop and see the wealth of resources available to Christians today. You can slim the Christian way, discover how to combat the devil's forces, learn about postmodernism or choose from all the latest Christian CDs. You will also see notices for celebrations, courses, praise meetings, special teaching days, and counselling services. You can deepen your theology, perform signs and wonders, and be blessed in a multitude of ways. But I do not see much on holiness. With so many other things going on it is easy to ignore holiness and I have to confess that is often what I have done.

Holiness – what's that?

'The greatest need of my congregation is my own personal holiness.' I still remember the first time I heard those words. I was on a rapid rise up the Christian leadership ladder. I had become a Christian just before going to university. I arrived at my college and eagerly joined the Christian Union. As I was the only first year who joined, so when the time came to appoint the leaders of the group in the college, I was the only one available! I had to learn about the Christian life and leadership very quickly. Then the college group occasionally went to local churches to lead services. I asked everyone else to preach at one of these services and they all refused – I was the only one available. I had to learn about preaching very quickly. Then I was 'promoted' to the post of prayer secretary leading a weekly prayer meeting of over a hundred fellow students.

Within two years of becoming a Christian I had become in my own mind a leader and a preacher, and began to feel God calling me to full-time work for the Church. I considered doing a theology degree. Perhaps I could work with an evangelist to build skills in that area. I devoured books on preaching and church growth. I became an 'authority' to fellow students on any charismatic phenomenon from speaking in tongues to casting out demons. God had given me the gifts. Now at the age of twenty I was ready to transform his Church(!).

One summer afternoon in a college room in Durham, a fellow student was commending various books to me. He was worried that I was becoming too 'happy-clappy' and thought I should read some 'proper' theology. One of the books was by a Scottish preacher called Robert Murray McCheyne. I'd never heard of him before but my friend who had recently read the book remembered his words, 'The greatest need of my congregation is my own personal holiness.' I nodded wisely to impress my friend. Yet I hadn't a clue what it meant. Surely the greatest need of a congregation is sound preaching or wise leadership or the ability to motivate others to share their faith. Yet the words kept coming back to me.

The 'success' continued. People responded to my preaching and became Christians. I preached in front of thousands at conventions. I worked with an eminent evangelist having opportunities way beyond my experience. I did a theology degree at Cambridge, wrote books and articles and was interviewed by the media. I developed a ministry in Christian apologetics and travelled widely. Yet through it all the words about holiness kept coming back.

It was not until I became a pastor of a church that I began to realise what Robert Murray McCheyne was on about. The 'success' as judged by Western Christian culture continued. We saw growth in numbers and Christian experience. New forms of multi-media worship were devised. People were sent out from the church to Estonia, Bangladesh, Papua New Guinea and Manila. A church plant was established in Liverpool city centre. People of all ages answered God's call to become ministers and preachers.

Yet I became more and more challenged about holiness. As I preached from the Bible, listened to my colleagues, studied the Bible on my own and in housegroups, the theme of holiness kept coming out again and again. I could not continue to ignore it. God seemed to be saying a very simple thing. Primarily, it did not matter to my church whether I could give the meaning of obscure Greek verbs, or how many TV or radio appearances I made or how many people responded to my evangelistic appeals. The greatest need was for me to live a holy life. More than that, God's priority for me was not to be a great evangelist or well-known Bible teacher but it was to be holy as God calls me to be holy.

I wish I could say for the sake of a dramatic story that I came to a crisis moment in my ministry, perhaps breaking down in the pulpit one morning. That, however, was not my experience. It was a very gradual process of deepening faith and changing priorities. Time after time my priorities were and still are wrong. Nevertheless I felt the gentle pressure of God's Spirit driving me back to the Bible to discover what it means to be holy. The fascinating thing was that as I began to explore what the Bible means by holiness, it was quite different to the view of holiness that I had grown up with in Christian circles. I had misunderstood what it means to be holy.

Holiness misunderstood

I ignored the importance of holiness because I misunderstood it. Instead of being the dynamic, practical, world-changing doctrine it is meant to be, I viewed it as boring, negative and totally out of touch with the world. To be holy, I thought, was to say 'no' to premarital sex, pray alone a lot and be very religious.

My understanding was controlled by four myths, none of which was true. They are that holiness is:

1. Individualistic

The popular impression of holiness is to become a hermit in the desert, or spend countless hours kneeling alone in prayer. I worried about this, not only because there are no deserts in Liverpool, but because it seemed selfish and solitary. Was it all just about me and God? The Bible's view seemed to be very different. Although prayer does play an essential part, holiness is not a lonely walk.

2. Self absorbed

Then there was the teaching that seemed to be all about 'casting out sin from the inner being and becoming pure'. It gave a picture of holiness which seemed to be about the self-examination of inner motives and thoughts, and the inner battle to conquer sin. But what about the world outside? The Bible did say that the inner life has an important part to play in holiness but it also emphasised the importance of outward action.

3. Unreal

Holiness is often presented as having little to do with everyday questions such as work, fashion or sex. In the children's television series *Postman Pat*, the local minister typifies such a view.

With dog collar and fluffy white hair, he is so out of touch with the world that he is entertaining but irrelevant to the real story. Not too far away are church leaders who today only seem to get headlines by saying 'no' to the National Lottery, genetic engineering or drugs. In many people's minds, the holy people seem to be totally divorced from and critical of this world. The Bible, however, was very different. It seemed to talk about holiness within the context of the real issues of the day. It was about being different from the world but not divorced from it.

4. Religious

Why do so many preachers and leaders of worship change the tone of their voices when they pray aloud? It has always fascinated me why their 'pulpit voice' is so different from their normal voice. This change of voice seems to be symptomatic of the view that to be holy is to appear religious.

Holiness is seen, in the words of one of my friends, as 'getting religion big time'. The holy person is the one at church at least three times on a Sunday, including washing up the coffee cups every week. The holy people should be serious about all things, with a face and voice which show just how holy they are. They have not got time for jokes, movies, 'loud music' or fashionable clothes. And their preferred topic of conversation is not last night's football match but 'what has the Lord been teaching you recently?'

To be honest such people scare me! More importantly they do not seem to reflect what the Bible says about holiness.

A different world?

There was a time in the Church when holiness was very popular and was a central concern to the life of a Christian. At the time of the Reformation, among the Puritans, and during the revivals in the eighteenth, nineteenth and twentieth centuries, holiness was promoted and understood. As I began to read Martin

Luther, John Calvin, John Owen, John Wesley, Andrew Murray and Amy Carmichael I entered a world of holiness. However, it is not just from the Protestant side of the Church. Orthodox and Roman Catholic writers and leaders such as Teresa of Avila also emphasised holiness.

However the trouble I had was that even getting over the different language, the world that these women and men of God lived in was very different to today. The founder of Methodism, John Wesley, seemed to say little about television, the environment or whether I should read tabloid newspapers. Of course God does not change, and human nature does not change, but if holiness is something about how we relate to the world, then a changing world needs a new understanding of holiness.

If holiness is not to be seen as irrelevant, then it needs to be thought about afresh by each new generation. More importantly it needs to be lived out with commitment and courage in each new generation.

Walking the tightrope

I've only tried to walk a tightrope once. It was at an outdoor playground and the rope was only six inches from the ground. Time after time I would fall. Time after time I would pick myself up, rub my bruises and try again. The most I managed was a few steps, but even that gave me a tremendous sense of achievement and exhilaration.

I often think about that experience. I plan in my head how I should place my feet for maximum balance. In my head I can be as good as I want, but that is not what it is about. For all the theory, ultimately you have to do it. You have to learn from experience, and that involves falling off. However, what I really needed to help me was an expert. Someone who was a good tightrope walker, someone to give me guidance and someone that I could hold on to as I developed.

To be holy is to walk a tightrope. In order to experience it you need to live it. You will make mistakes and fall along the way. The exciting truth of Christianity is that there is a helper and teacher who walks with you. He is the one to look to for guidance. He will be the one who picks you up and holds you up. For he is the risen Lord Jesus.

The image of walking a tightrope is helpful in another sense. To be holy is to take this truth of the Bible, listen to what it has meant to Christians of past generations, and then allow it to speak to the world of today. We need to value our past, whether our own history or the understanding of fellow Christians. But it is also about understanding this new world. To one side we can fall into the sub-culture of churchianity, becoming totally detached from the world. To the other side we can fall into the sub-culture of the world, totally enveloped by its values and lifestyles.

It is a long way from Steps to Bob Dylan. Recently I have been listening to the 'Royal Albert Hall' concert of 1966, a defining moment in rock history, at least for people who are as old as me. Actually recorded in Manchester, it features part of the tour when Dylan plugged in his electric guitar and unleashed a new sound. Many did not want to hear that new sound, preferring to stay with the familiar folk music of an earlier Dylan. At one point a fan calls out, 'Judas'. Dylan's response was to launch into a song which would become one of the all time classics, 'Like a Rolling Stone'. Dylan felt that the power of his poetry, so loved by the folk fanatics, needed to be reformulated for a new world. He was walking a tightrope on that tour.

This book is an attempt to re-express biblical holiness for a new generation. But it comes out of a personal story of many mistakes and yet a growing hunger for real holiness. My prayer is that as you read the book, and in particular as you study the passages of Scripture, so your life may be changed – to become more holy.

So what is holiness?

Each chapter of this book explores a different aspect of holiness within the Bible. The first part of the book sets out the basics of the doctrine and then the second and third parts work out what it means to be holy in terms of an individual life and the world.

In all of this the Bible is of central importance for me. Each chapter is tied to a biblical passage (or passages). The reasons for this are both personal and pastoral. I have read many books on holiness but they offer little compared to what I have discovered about holiness through simply reading the Bible. As a pastor of a church I have found this to be true not just for me but for many others. I could provide brilliant illustrations and preach with great technique, but only as we allow God to speak through his word are people made more holy. This means that rather than a logical detailing of the doctrine of holiness, the biblical picture of holiness is slowly built up through each chapter. Although each chapter is self contained in terms of the issue it addresses, to build up an understanding of holiness you have to read them all.

The word 'holy' when applied to people in both Hebrew and Greek means separated and set apart for God. It is to reflect his character. The writer John White puts it thus: 'holiness is to be and to act like God.'[1] Yet the Christian faith proclaims a God who, though separated from us in his quality of perfection, justice and love, is the same God who becomes involved in our world in Jesus.

This is the tightrope we have to walk. How can we be different but involved? Each chapter explores how we might walk this tightrope. At the end of each chapter there is a Study and Action guide on how you might go further:

One book to read: Suggests a book that you may want to buy or borrow to go into the issues in more depth. Each of the chapters is only an introduction.

One outline for discussion: You may want to use this book in a housegroup or cell group, or simply want to talk over the issues with a Christian friend. The questions are designed to open up the area for discussion, rather than having a short 'right' answer. Furthermore, this section asks the questions in the context of local church life.

One question for yourself: As you read the Bible you might feel God is speaking to you, challenging you to change or affirming things you have already learnt. It is good to pray about these things and this question can be used as a way in to prayer.

One action to take: God wants specific responses from us when we read his word. This action is simply a suggestion. It may not be the best for you, but it might help you to think through your own course of action in response to what God is saying.

Notes

1. John White, *Holiness* (Eagle: Guildford, 1996), p. 7.

PART ONE
The Basics

1

THE BIG HOLY ONE

The trouble with religious language is that at times it is very difficult to understand what it means. In a recent street survey members of the public were asked to define various religious terms. When asked what 'adultery' was, someone replied that it was the sin of saying that you were older than you really were. 'Begotten' was defined as the opposite of forgotten, and 'consecrate' was defined as something they do to coconuts! When it came to the word 'holiness' most people had nothing to say at all, apart from one person who said 'something the Pope has prayed for'.

Many Christians today would also be at a loss to define holiness, and really understand what it means. Its root meaning is 'to separate' or 'to set apart' and when applied to God speaks of his moral excellence, his purity and the fact that he is different from us. However, it is very easy for us to see this in negative terms. Often when we apply the word 'holiness' to God we see an image in our minds of God as remote and far from us. Or we see God as a God of religious observance, forever checking our lives for the slightest sign of impurity. The headmaster of my school was rarely seen. You only saw him if you were very, very bad or very, very good. Before I experienced Jesus I saw God like that. We then transfer such an image to a 'holy' person whom we often see as someone totally isolated from the world.

How do we get a true picture of God? Paul states it quite clearly when he writes that Christ 'is the image of the invisible God' (Col 1:15). In answer to the question 'What is God like?' Christians reply he is like Jesus. That is why the New Testament Gospels can teach us so much about holiness. Indeed the holiness of God which we see in Jesus is not about a remote and negative God, but is positive and exciting.

Take for example the following passage:

[1]One day as Jesus was standing by the Lake of Gennesaret, with the people crowding round him and listening to the word of God, [2]he saw at the water's edge two boats, left there by the fishermen, who were washing their nets. [3]He got into one of the boats, the one belonging to Simon, and asked him to put out a little from shore. Then he sat down and taught the people from the boat.

[4]When he had finished speaking, he said to Simon, 'Put out into deep water, and let down the nets for a catch.'

[5]Simon answered, 'Master, we've worked hard all night and haven't caught anything. But because you say so, I will let down the nets.'

[6]When they had done so, they caught such a large number of fish that their nets began to break. [7]So they signalled to their partners in the other boat to come and help them, and they came and filled both boats so full that they began to sink.

[8]When Simon Peter saw this, he fell at Jesus' knees and said, 'Go away from me, Lord; I am a sinful man!' [9]For he and all his companions were astonished at the catch of fish they had taken, [10]and so were James and John, the sons of Zebedee, Simon's partners.

Then Jesus said to Simon, 'Don't be afraid; from now on you will catch men and women.' [11]So they pulled their boats up on shore, left everything and followed him'

(Luke 5:1–11)

In his Gospel Luke has already given us a clue to the holiness of God in Jesus. The angel says to Mary that 'the holy one to be born will be called the Son of God' (Lk 1:35), and then the demon in the Capernaum synagogue says to Jesus, 'I know who you are – the Holy One of God' (Lk 4:34).

However, in this story of the calling of the disciples and the miraculous catch of fish, we see it most clearly. Simon Peter falls before Jesus and says, 'Go away from me, Lord; I am a sinful man!' (v8). It is a similar response to when the prophet Isaiah saw the holiness of God (Is 6:1–7). The New Testament scholar Howard Marshall comments, 'Simon was overwhelmed with a sense of the holiness of Jesus as Lord.'[1]

But what sort of picture do we get of this holiness? If we read Luke's account carefully, it is perhaps not what we might expect.

1. Everyday holiness

This account says that God's holiness is encountered in an ordinary, everyday event by ordinary, everyday people. Now you might say that a miraculous catch of fish is not an ordinary event, but in focusing on miracles we often forget to see the context. For this revelation of the holiness of God did not happen in the Temple, or during a praise time at the Pharisees' summer convention, or in the spiritual capital of Jerusalem. It happened to some blokes who were fishing.

The scene is the Sea of Galilee with fishermen washing their nets. After a night's fishing, the boring bit needed to be done. The nets would need cleaning and repairing. Because of the size of the crowd, Jesus asks Simon if he can use his boat as a make-shift pulpit. Then in typical rabbinic style he sits down and teaches. After he has finished teaching, Jesus decides to pay Simon for using his boat.

Jesus says to Simon, 'Put out into deep water, and let down the nets for a catch' (v4). Now Simon does not say, 'O great and wise one, I would be blessed beyond measure to do this.' Simon's immediate reaction is much more natural. 'We've worked hard all night and haven't caught anything!' Roughly translated, 'Jesus, you cannot be serious! Look, we're tired, we want to go home for something to eat. We didn't catch anything last night, and with respect what does a preacher know about fishing? You want us to go out during the day? We'd be a laughing stock!' Simon, however, for whatever reason gives in and does as he is told.

There is a lesson here for Simon Peter. God's holiness was invading his private life. Perhaps he could cope with Jesus as the religious rabbi. But when that rabbi got into the boat, that was a different matter. When Jesus started to get involved in his fishing, where he and not the preacher was the expert, Simon's universe was upset.

God's holiness is not remote. The God of the Bible is in the here and now. David Jenkins describes God as 'transcendence in the midst'. There is a grubbiness to God's holiness in the sense that his purity and love can be experienced in the dirt, the pain, the everyday of this world.

I see this most of all in the way this holy God became flesh. Born in the outhouse of a pub, to unimportant parents, in an outback corner of the Roman empire, to a people who were oppressed politically and depressed spiritually. A man who lived in virtual obscurity for thirty years not in Jerusalem but in Nazareth. His first sermon was at his home synagogue in Nazareth, where he was rejected by his own people and family. He heals unnamed people like Simon's mother-in-law, he spends time with women, tax collectors and prostitutes, and he puts his trust in a number of disciples who fail him at every point. He does not separate himself from the world, but touches lepers, allows a sinful woman to anoint his feet, and he weeps with compassion. In the end he endures rejection, mocking, cruelty, pain, violence and even death by torture on a cross. This is the holy God.

Now the meaning of this often neglected view of God's holiness is profound. It means, first, that God is accessible. Of course, our rebellion from God does cut us off from God, just as walking away from someone ends the conversation. But God is always taking the initiative in reaching out to us and revealing himself to us. Malcolm Muggeridge was a journalist who was converted to the Christian faith not primarily by brilliant argument but by seeing in the work of Mother Theresa something more than just a caring individual. He encountered God's holiness in the dirt, pain and suffering of the streets of Calcutta – and it changed his life.

A friend of mine at university was an atheist. He would talk to a number of us who were Christians about God but all our arguments would seem to hit a brick wall. After one vacation he proudly announced he had become a Christian. I eagerly asked him how it had happened, expecting him to say something like, 'Well, I thought about your arguments again. . . .', or 'I went to your church and the worship was just so great. . . .' In fact he replied, 'Well, I had nothing to do over Easter, I was bored, and so started to watch the film *Ben Hur* on television. By the end of the movie I was a Christian.' My initial reaction was to say, 'That just cannot happen!' But it did.

If you are searching for God, or trying to return to him after a period of rebellion, he may reach out to you in a special mission or celebration, or he may reach out to you in everyday life. Faced with a holy God we need to remember that as we ask the question 'how do I, a sinner, approach God?' – God is actually approaching us.

It means, secondly, that our holiness needs to be everyday holiness. It is not just about church on a Sunday, or a prayer meeting, or a Bible study. Holiness should pervade the whole of our lives. Too often holiness is presented as an image hiding the true reality.

As a minister, you quickly learn you have a strange effect on people. I visited a couple the other day and as I walked down the drive I could hear them having a blazing row. I wondered about turning away, but pressed on and rang the doorbell. The row continued down the corridor until the point when the door was opened. An angry face immediately turned into a serene smile. The husband said, 'Oh, good morning, do come in.' Then he called, 'Darling, the minister is here.' His wife then appeared with a beaming smile, 'Do come in. Would you like some tea?' 'Oh, let me make it, darling,' the husband said. As I left the house I heard the voices rising again!

The holiness which God asks of us is not characterised by being seen at the all-night prayer vigil, but whether it makes a difference to the pressure points of life, that is our attitudes to sex, relationships, our use of money, pride and ambition. Are we holy in the honesty and integrity we show in our work or even in filling out tax returns?

2. Attractive holiness

The result of Simon Peter following the instructions of Jesus was that they caught such a large catch of fish that their nets began to break (v6). It was a very good way to repay them for the use of the boat. What could be more attractive to fishermen, not only that they should have the biggest catch of their lives, but that it should happen right in front of all of their fellow fishermen (v7)! This demonstration of God's holiness was a positive and attractive event.

At times we all dream about being like someone else. When I play soccer I wish I was like Alan Shearer. I wish I could sing like Bono, have the comic timing of Stephen Fry and cook like Delia Smith. Those who know me realise just how much of a dreamer I am! However, in the end there is only one person that I would wish to be like. I want to be like the one who spent forty days in the wilderness and was still able to resist the devil. The one who freed people by casting out evil spirits, who brings healing and dignity to those rejected by others. The one who condemns sin but loves the sinner, and who is able to turn the tables on those who would try and catch him out. Supremely, I wish I was like the one who gave his life for others. The one who loved the friends who rejected him, who loved those who reviled, tortured and abused him. The one who in his own agony on the cross had time to say to a thief, 'Today you will be with me in paradise', and to say, before his enemies, 'Father, forgive them, they don't know what they do.' I want to be like that person. For all that is good, all that is humanity at its best, all that is attractive – is in that person. Dostoevsky once wrote, 'I believe there is no one lovelier, deeper, more sympathetic and more perfect than Jesus.'

God's perfection is not a negative thing. There is a delight about perfection. That perfect golf shot that you've been waiting years for, that perfect meal when the recipe turns out just as it appears in the picture. There is something good and attractive about perfection.

This means two things also. First, it is important that we hang on to this in a world which is often ugly. In the last week here in Liverpool I have driven past the shopping centre where the toddler James Bulger was abducted and killed by other children, and a block of flats where Kosovan refugees are about to be housed. I have wept with a person whose relationships are falling apart. I have sat beside a man dying an awful death through cancer. I do not know why such things happen. I am sad and angry and often overwhelmed by the mess this world is in. I find myself questioning why God allows it. In such times I can only cling on to the fact that the God I see revealed in Jesus is about goodness, love and extravagant generosity.

Second, our holiness needs to be attractive. The Christian martyr John Bradford received the nickname 'Holy Bradford'. Aware of his own falling short of what God would have him do, he signed all his letters, 'A most miserable sinner, John Bradford.' One cannot help to speculate on whether he used this form when he sent birthday greetings, or letters of love to his fiancée! Our image of a holy person is often someone who speaks in religious language, is judgemental of all, and is miserable. But being holy is really about being fully human. It is about being the person God wants you to be. James Philip wrote, 'The greatest saints of God have been characterised not by halos and an atmosphere of distant unapproachability, but by their humanity.'[2]

The world will say that to be an attractive person you need to be sexy, powerful, put other people down and have lots of money. The gospel says that this is a lie. Following Jesus and finding your true humanity as you do so, makes you an attractive person.

3. Compelling holiness

When Simon Peter saw the catch of fish and realised what was going on, his reaction was extreme. He fell at Jesus' feet, acknowledged Jesus as Lord and that he was a sinful man, and then asked Jesus to depart from him (v8). This was natural. He was overwhelmed by his own inadequacy when faced with the power of Jesus. The holy love of God does not simply give you a warm feeling in the pit of your stomach, akin to a fluffy bunny Valentine card. It often leads to a sense of fear, and a recognition of the need for repentance.

I think I know how Simon Peter felt. There have been moments in my own life when I have not wanted to be in the presence of Jesus. Recently, I was leading a very traditional service and I was praying aloud. As I prayed I began to get a glimpse of the beauty of God and a sense of my own unworthiness. I wanted to run out of the church during my own prayer! It was just too much. However, Jesus does not leave Simon Peter there. He does *not* let the sinner depart from him. He says to Simon Peter, 'Don't be afraid' (v10) and then calls him into the close relationship of discipleship. The offer of forgiveness and acceptance is then followed by the call to be part of his mission. Right at the point of Simon's running away, Jesus meets him and calls him.

Many writers speak of God's holiness as his wrath against sin. In that they are correct. But this is not a God who gives the sinner a good telling off and then leaves him or her there.

As a student I went to a meeting where a local vicar was talking about the baptism in the Holy Spirit. It was not a large gathering and so we were sitting around in a circle. The vicar made the claim that he could always tell if someone was baptised in the Spirit (and by implication living a good spiritual life), by simply looking into their eyes. At this point all twenty pairs of eyes found the carpet most interesting, and did so for the rest of the evening! There are some brothers and sisters in the Church who frighten me. Their encouragement to greater Christian commitment and holiness often leaves me with more guilt than enthusiasm.

However, there are other sisters and brothers who so demonstrate the holiness of God in graciousness, gentleness, love and encouragement, that you just cannot help being drawn or compelled into it. Greater Christian commitment almost flows naturally. God's holiness is like that. He condemns sin, but his love and grace are about drawing the sinner into a closer walk with himself. Reg was an old Salvation Army leader who began to come to our church's luncheon club. He 'oozed' holiness. But his holiness never condemned others. It acted as an encouragement to be holy. He once said to me that God gives us a crown and then helps us to grow into it.

This holiness which draws us in, compels us to change. There was a time when shops which sold women's clothes had no relevance to me at all. These days I go into them regularly and have worked out the subtle differences between Dorothy Perkins and Next. The reason, I quickly add, is that I am now married and my wife has introduced me to a whole new world. As we experience the holiness of God, so this compels us to experience a whole new world, where we see and share his concerns.

Simon Peter was invited to change, to become not a fisherman on the Sea of Galilee, but a fisher of men and women throughout the world. It was a change which would be difficult, but ultimately the most satisfying thing in the world. It was his experience of the holiness of God as he encountered it in Jesus that made the difference.

The writer of the letter to the Hebrews sees the purpose of God as so 'we may share in his holiness' (Heb 12:10). It is something that God wants for us all. Because God is holy, so we should be holy. Simon Peter had begun to learn that in his encounter with Jesus. Later in his life, he wrote in one of his letters: 'But just as he who called you is holy, so be holy in all you do; for it is written: "Be holy, because I am holy"' (1 Pet 1:15–16).

Study and Action

One book to read: J. I. Packer, *A Passion for Holiness* (Crossway Books: Nottingham, 1992).

One outline for discussion:

1. How important is the subject of holiness in your local fellowship – in teaching and preaching, in appointing leaders, in prayer and in worship?
2. Have you encountered the holiness of God in a similar way to Simon Peter?
3. Do you find it hard to put God at the centre of everyday life – in work, relationships or use of money?
4. Do you fear God's holiness, and why?

One question for yourself: What area of your life does God want to change?

One action to take: Put aside an extra two minutes a day to pray.

Notes

1. I. H. Marshall, *Luke* (Paternoster: Exeter, 1978), p. 134.
2. J. Philip, *Christian Maturity* (IVP: London, 1964), p. 70.

2

HOLY TRANSFORMATION OR WHOLLY RELIGIOUS?

For some of us the term 'punk rock' brings back rather embarrassing teenage memories! It was a movement in popular music and culture which originated in the 1970s. Groups like The Sex Pistols, The Ramones and The Clash advocated anarchy, attacked the class system and monarchy, and embodied a youth anger at certain features of Western culture. In fashion, designers such as Vivian Westwood exhibited the same energy, and leather jackets, safety pins and zips became identifying badges. The gurus of this movement such as Malcolm Maclaren pontificated on a new revolution.

The trouble was that this revolution never really came. Punk eventually became a victim of the very forces of commercialism and materialism which it fought. The music is now used to sell jeans in TV ads, and in London postcards of punks are in the same rack as Diana, Princess of Wales. However, its importance should not be dismissed. It highlighted, especially from the young, a cry of being stranded and alienated. It looked for a new beginning in celebrating cynicism and searched for liberation in self-destruction.

By a quirk of radio programming, a feature on punk on a recent radio show was immediately followed by advice on when to plant tulips! The contrast of the two items was stark. In terms of planting tulips, life goes on each year in its same old traditional pattern.

It struck me that this contrast was a reflection on society. There are those who hunger after a new beginning, who realise that there is something wrong with themselves and the world and try to do something about it. Then there are those for whom life goes on as it always did. Nothing needs to be changed. Fitting into the system, trying to live a good life, perhaps going to church, and planting tulips is how it should be.

In John 3, in the encounter of Jesus with Nicodemus, Jesus addresses both of these kinds of people. To the 'tulip growers' he says that they need to have a new beginning. To the 'punks' he says that such a new beginning cannot be achieved by themselves. Such an understanding is foundational to biblical holiness.

Now there was a man of the Pharisees named Nicodemus, a member of the Jewish ruling council. [2]He came to Jesus at night and said, 'Rabbi, we know you are a teacher who has come from God. For no-one could perform the miraculous signs you are doing if God were not with him.'

[3]In reply Jesus declared, 'I tell you the truth, no-one can see the kingdom of God unless he is born again.'

[4]How can a man be born when he is old?' Nicodemus asked. 'Surely he cannot enter a second time into his mother's womb to be born!'

[5]Jesus answered, 'I tell you the truth, no-one can enter the kingdom of God unless he is born of water and the Spirit. [6]Flesh gives birth to flesh, but the Spirit gives birth to spirit. [7]You should not be surprised at my saying, "You must be born again." [8]The wind blows wherever it pleases. You hear its sound, but you cannot tell where it comes from or where it is going. So it is with everyone born of the Spirit.'

[9]'How can this be?' Nicodemus asked.

[10]'You are Israel's teacher,' said Jesus, 'and do you not understand these things?'

(John 3:1–10)

1. A new beginning is needed by all

Most of us think that a new start is needed by only some. We would point our finger at drug addicts, adulterers, racists, thieves and no doubt a few friends of ours whose lives, in our Christian estimation, could do with a little improvement. If we were to suggest who in John's Gospel really needed a new start we might think of the woman of Samaria (Jn 4), or the woman caught in adultery (Jn 8) or even Pilate (Jn 19). At a human level, we look upon the 'unholy' people as requiring radical transformation.

It is against this background that Jesus makes a powerful point. For who is it, in the whole of John's Gospel, that Jesus talks to on this matter? Nicodemus is probably the last person we would have expected. John tells us three things about this man. First, he was 'a man of the Pharisees' (v1). He was a member of the Jewish religious party who were strict in obedience to the law, not just in the Temple but in everyday life. Indeed, they attempted to bring the purity of the Temple into everyday life. They were attempting to live holy lives. Ritual cleanliness, tithing, fasting twice a week, and regular prayer would be fundamental to the life of Nicodemus. Christians have often given Pharisees a bad press, representing them all as evil and corrupt. This is not the case: many Pharisees gave of themselves in an attempt to be right with God. In our day Nicodemus would be seen as someone sick with religion, a member of the 'God Squad'. He would be the one always at the prayer meeting, the first to give money to worthwhile causes and would always say grace before meals, even in public restaurants!

Second, he was 'a member of the Jewish ruling council' (v1). He was a member of the Jewish council of Pharisees and chief priests for John tells us later in his Gospel that when this group met to plot against Jesus, Nicodemus advised caution (Jn 7:45–52). Some have suggested that it was because of this,

Nicodemus came to Jesus at night in order that he would not be seen as representing the official Jewish line. Whatever the reason, Nicodemus had power and prestige beyond simply being a religious man.

Third, he was 'Israel's teacher' (v10). Nicodemus was the teacher in Israel. He probably had four degrees, was a professor of theology and a regular contributor to Radio Jerusalem's 'Thought for the Day'! So Nicodemus had a good moral character, he had influence and power and he had great learning. What else did he need? Something, however, brought him to Jesus. Possibly it was his active mind, or possibly it was to check Jesus out. He came by night and speaks of miracles and what they represent (v2). But Jesus has a more important topic to speak about. Jesus goes to the heart of the issue and speaks about how a person can belong to and experience the kingdom of God.

Jesus says that for this to happen a person must be 'born again' (or born anew). It is an image of a totally new beginning. Such a term could be used in horticulture when a new species evolves or in history when a new era begins. To enter into the kingdom of God needs an equivalent change in the life of an individual. That this conversation happens with Nicodemus sharpens the point. It does not matter how religious, how powerful, how intellectual you are, to experience the kingly rule of God you must be born again.

'Tulip growing' in religion and life is not enough. Of course there is much to commend faithfulness and diligence in prayer, study and doing good works. But this is not biblical holiness. Religion has a habit of making us too comfortable.

As part of a mission tour I once found myself preaching at a packed church. I preached my heart out, and after the final prayer of the service, bowed my head in the pulpit for a brief prayer asking God to forgive my failures and make the message bear fruit. When I opened my eyes, half of the church was already empty and there were so many people in the aisles that

I could not get to the door to say good-bye to folk. I was worried that I had said something which had offended but the minister assured me that this happened every week. He said, 'Once they've done their hour per week and eased their guilt, that's all they want.' Their religion of a weekly church service made them feel better but they were never getting beyond that.

Holiness begins with the realisation of the need for a radical new beginning, to be born again.

2. This new beginning is spiritual

Nicodemus, however, just cannot grasp this 'new beginning'. He replies , 'How can a man be born when he is old? Surely he cannot enter a second time into his mother's womb to be born?'(v4). He has a good point. Nicodemus is saying that his life is a process, it is the result of biological and psychological changes. To be born again would require something quite extraordinary.

Jesus replies that he is right, something quite extraordinary is needed. But Nicodemus is thinking about this too literally. To be born again is to receive a spiritual new beginning. It is at this point that Jesus introduces the Spirit. He seems to suggest that being born of water is not enough. Some commentators take this as referring to physical birth from the womb, others take it as referring to the baptism of John for repentance. A person needs to be born of the Spirit, for only this birth can lead to spiritual life. For all his great learning and religion, Nicodemus has missed the need for an inner spiritual change.

As it is from the Spirit, we cannot bring this change our-selves. The imagery reinforces that. Birth is not something we can achieve by ourselves! In addition the very term 'born again' can be translated 'born from above'. The way into the kingdom of God is not primarily by keeping the law, it is by receiving the Spirit's gift of inner renewal. Campbell Morgan calls it a 'new life principle', while J. C. Ryle writes of it as 'calling into existence a new creature, with a new nature, new habits of life, new tastes, new judgments, new opinions, new hopes and fears'.

Nicodemus, however, is still struggling to grasp this. So Jesus tells him to think about the wind. The wind is mysterious in where it comes from and where it goes but you experience its effects. So it is with one born of the Spirit. You may not be able to fully understand it, but you can experience it and see its effects.

Punk was right in the need for a radical new beginning, but wrong in assuming that this revolution could be achieved by ourselves. Victor Hugo, commenting on the French revolution, said that revolution can change everything, except the human heart. Jesus is saying that only a spiritual revolution can provide a true new beginning.

This is important if you despair of ever changing. You may see the need for change but have tried many things without success. Philosophy, religion or personal discipline have not led to lasting change but simply a sense of failure and guilt. You have started to believe that nothing can change human nature. Into this situation Jesus says: there is hope. For what is impossible for humans is possible with God.

Mark arrived at our Christmas carol service with bottles of pills ready to take his own life. Having rejected the Christian faith of his school and parents, he had endured a number of tough things but had come to the end of himself. In his desperation he came to church. God touched him during the service. It was not a dramatic experience but something happened. At the end of the service he gave me the pills and we talked. In the next few weeks his life showed a dramatic change. When we talked after the Christmas holiday I could not believe that I was talking to the same person. In one sense I was not. God had brought the profound change that he desired, leading to joy, valuing himself, getting a new purpose in life and serving others.

That God can change lives in this way is an important truth to be grasped for those who desire to lead a holy life. Holiness from beginning to end is a work of God in us and through us. It is not about us working ourselves up into a spiritual frenzy, buying books on 'Holy Living Today – 1001 tips for a good life', and deciding to live away from any temptation for 100 years. The beginning of holiness is to be born anew by the Spirit of God and receive this radical transformation. Holiness is then by God's daily help living in this new relationship.

John White puts it like this, 'God had set me free to walk the path of holiness.' This freedom, or this new start is offered to us though the death and resurrection of Jesus. As the conversation with Nicodemus moves to its conclusion, Jesus begins to speak about his own death. He likens it to an incident in the history of Israel which Nicodemus would know well. Numbers 21:4–9 tells of when the people of Israel in the wilderness rebelled against God. The result of that rebellion was that poisonous snakes began to attack the people, and as they cried out to God, Moses was instructed to make a model of a snake on a pole. If people looked at this snake lifted up on the pole then they would be saved.

Jesus speaks about his own 'lifting up', that is his death on the cross, in the same way. As people look, believe and trust, so they are saved from condemnation to eternal life. But how does this happen?

3. This new beginning is arrived at by different people in different ways

As John's account continues, it is then not clear whether the words of Jesus continue or if John himself comments on Jesus (vv16–21). However, what is clear is that Nicodemus fades out of the narrative almost as quickly as he came into it. The impression that is left is that Nicodemus goes away somewhat puzzled.

We next meet him in the report of the plotting of the chief priests and Pharisees against Jesus (Jn 7:45–52). Nicodemus reminds them of the law, that they should not condemn without first giving a hearing. The response is sharp and dismissive. 'You're not one of them from Galilee, are you! If you really looked into it, you wouldn't be so stupid', or words to that effect. Nicodemus disappears from the narrative again.

The final glimpse of Nicodemus is much later, in fact after the death of Jesus (Jn 19:39–42). This time Nicodemus finally gets off the fence and puts his life where his thoughts have been taking him. John tells us that with Joseph of Arimathea, it was Nicodemus who prepared the body of Jesus for burial. This is a tremendously public act for someone like Nicodemus. It is perhaps at this late stage that his discipleship becomes real. If this is the case, then it has taken sixteen chapters for Nicodemus to make up his mind!

Donald English has pointed out the contrast of Nicodemus' faith journey to other characters in John's Gospel. For example, instead of taking sixteen chapters, Nathanael seems to make up his mind in a few verses (Jn 1:43–51).[1] His response when Philip tells him of Jesus is not exactly enthusiastic: 'Can anything good come from Nazareth?' More of an 'Eeyore' than a 'Tigger' response! Yet after a short conversation with Jesus he is transformed to proclaim, 'Rabbi, you are the Son of God.'

In addition, contrast the woman of Samaria (Jn 4:1–42), with questioning Thomas (Jn 11:16; 14:5, 20:24–31), and with tearful Mary (Jn 11:28–37). The woman of Samaria engages in deep theological discussion, Thomas wants to ask the obvious questions, and Mary is simply overcome with emotion. Put all of these people together and what do we see? The common theme is that they all respond to Jesus. Indeed, for John that is the key to salvation and the beginning of the road of holiness. But they do so in different ways.

It is always amazing for me to see how different people begin this journey. Nick was staying with his grandmother when he felt he needed to find out about Jesus. She was a good Methodist and, unsure of what to do in such an unexpected situation, she decided to call the Methodist minister! She phoned and said to me, 'Could you please come round now and convert my grandson.' It was not a normal request! We had been talking for only twenty minutes when he asked whether he could become a Christian. I felt a little frustrated as I was only halfway through my explanation of the Christian faith! But there in his grandmother's living room he asked Jesus to come into his life. In contrast, Mike met with me weekly for nearly a year, asking questions, going over everything in fine detail and being ultra cautious about any public commitment. I am thrilled that they are both committed Christians wanting to live holy lives, and reminded that God's ways are not my ways.

Some need time, some have an instant response, some need to ask the questions, some are overcome with emotion. New birth happens in different ways in different people. At the birth of our son, my wife's labour was so short that there was no time for her to receive pain relief and I nearly missed the birth! Someone else we know was in labour for three days. Both gave birth to new life but in very different ways.

Donald English comments, ' We must not rush ahead of the patient urgency of the Spirit's action in the life of another person.' If we recognise that the Holy Spirit does not work in the rather neat simplistic way we would like, then we might be better helpers to those who look for and experience this new beginning on the path of holiness. We might also recognise and thank God for what he has done in our lives. Often because we do not fit other people's experience or model we sometimes doubt that we have been truly born again. This can especially be the case if we have grown up with our Christian faith, or do not have one 'conversion experience' that we can recall. What is important is not whether we can remember our birth, it is whether we are alive.

To walk a tightrope you need to make that first step. It is a step of trust. In *Indiana Jones and the Last Crusade*, Harrison Ford's character comes to the final obstacle before reaching the

Holy Grail. It seems to be a vast chasm without any way to get across. His 'clues' on how to get across tell him to step out and trust. Only as he takes that first step does he find the ledge which is there, obscured until he takes the step of faith.

I often find myself struggling with uncertainty and fear. Yet God asks us to step forward with him and he has never let me down.

Study and Action

One book to read: J. C. Ryle, *Holiness* (Evangelical Press: Herts, England, 1979).

One outline for discussion:
1. Share how God has brought you to this point in your Christian life.
2. How do we use religion to feel comfortable?
3. What do you want to change in your life?
4. Why do we find it difficult if people have a different experience of God to us?

One question for yourself: How much do you rely on yourself rather than God?

One action to take: Make some kind of representation of your Christian life so far. It may be a written account, it may be a diagram, it may be a painting or poem. Share it with one close Christian friend.

Notes

1. Donald English, *The Meaning of the Warmed Heart* (Methodist Publishing House: Peterborough, 1988).

3

ISOLATED HERMIT OR HOLY INVOLVEMENT?

What would life be like without television? I cannot get through the week without a weekly dose of *The Simpsons*, *Star Trek* and some kind of sport whether it be football or cricket. I find myself switching on the television at other times for no apparent reason, my index finger finding some kind of comfort in flicking through channels to the annoyance of everyone else. Indeed, on average each person in the UK watches 24 hours of television per week. That means in seventy years, we will spend ten years of solid television watching. And I have to say I am not too far away from the average.

There are those of course who refuse to have television. Some argue that it is a waste of time and money, while others argue against it on far more fundamental grounds. They believe that the language, hype, and underlying philosophy of a materialistic worldview can pollute the home environment.

In the UK it has been a particular concern of Christians that over the past decade there has been a fall in moral standards and an erosion of any space on television or radio for Christian programmes. Religious programmes seem to be sidelined to the early morning or late night slots. I once did a programme for the BBC for Christmas Day which because of the big movies could only be watched in the early hours of Boxing Day morning!

While less time is given to Christian programmes on the main terrestrial channels, there are new opportunities through new technology. The multi-channel revolution of satellite, cable and digital broadcasting has both negative and positive features. Extreme sex and violence can be accommodated on one channel while other channels can be owned and programmed by Christian groups.

In the past few years, the UK has followed the US model with a Christian radio station and attempts at Christian TV channels. This may be inevitable in terms of the future of broadcasting. But I do worry about it. Will the Christian faith become just a minority interest channel, on a par with the comedy channel or the science fiction channel? Will Christian media professionals leave the main networks and find haven in the sub-culture of Christian television and radio? And if they do, who will stand for what is right in the secular world?

To raise this issue in the context of holiness highlights a deeper question. As holy people what is our attitude to the world? Or how do we make the world holy? There are those extreme understandings of holiness which say that Christians should have as little to do with the world as possible. They should not allow themselves to be polluted by the images and assumptions of secular television or music. They should not be compromised by working in a non-Christian environment. Such a view is not too far away from what began to happen in the fourth century. Christian monks became hermits. Off they went into the desert or sat on top of pillars, so they could be separated from the temptations of this world and have time and space to develop the spiritual disciplines of prayer, meditation, fasting and inward examination. Such a life was viewed as a holy life. In the Middle Ages such a view of holiness was promoted for those who wanted to be serious about God, the super-Christians.

If that is extreme, this view of holiness is still around today, although in a more subtle form. It is attractive to those who want to be serious with God. I sometimes think that it would be better to be away from all temptation. Prayer would be much easier if I didn't have small children interrupting me or the thought of the football match or soap opera on the television. Some of my friends sometimes say that if only they lived in a Christian community or worked in a Christian company, then it would be easier to be holy.

Now, of course, there is a very real sense in which God calls some to a life of prayer, service and at times solitude. But this is not the call to holy living given to all Christians.

The following passage of the Bible reminds me of the importance of not being isolated but about being involved. It is part of Jesus' great block of teaching in Matthew's Gospel which we commonly refer to as the sermon on the mount:

> [13]'You are the salt of the earth. But if the salt loses its saltiness, how can it be made salty again? It is no longer good for anything, except to be thrown out and trampled by men.
> [14]You are the light of the world. A city on a hill cannot be hidden. [15]Neither do people light a lamp and put it under a bowl. Instead they put it on its stand, and it gives light to everyone in the house. [16]In the same way, let your light shine before men, that they may see your good deeds and praise your Father in heaven.'
>
> (Matthew 5:13–16)

Martin Lloyd Jones was minister of Westminster Chapel in London for a number of years and became famous for his expository preaching. He had a strong emphasis on the importance of holiness, Bible study and prayer. I had heard of his reputation and thought that he was quite puritanical and critical of the world. I remember seeing a photograph of him with his family on the beach – he sat wearing a dark suit and hat! Yet when I began to read his sermons, his view of holiness was not about separation from the world. He commented on these verses: 'The whole error of monasticism (was) that living the Christian life meant of necessity separating oneself from society and living a life of contemplation. Now that is something which is denied everywhere in the Scriptures, and nowhere more completely than in this verse.'[1]

Jesus begins with a very emphatic 'you'. It has the sense of you and you alone. Although the crowds are around it is not the crowds he addresses. He sat down and 'his disciples came to him, and he began to teach them' (Mt 5:1–2). He begins with what are called the beatitudes, descriptions of what it means to be a disciple. It is his followers that he is talking to. Notice that he says 'you are'. He does not say, 'you will be if you show me whether I can trust you', or 'you can be'. To say of his disciples 'you are salt' and 'you are light' are not promises but statements. They are images which we need to explore.

1. The salt of the earth

The image of salt that we have in our minds in the late twentieth century could be its chemical formula, its use in cooking or its use in being sprayed from the back of a lorry onto roads that are icy.

What would have come into the minds of the disciples in first-century Palestine? The first obvious picture is that salt is the 'enemy of decay'. It was used as a preservative, being rubbed into the meat to stop it decaying. Salt preserves the good and stops decay. To be 'salt of the earth' is therefore to keep wholesome what is good in society, and to oppose what is corrupt. It is very easy for Christians to judge and condemn society for many things – breakdown of relationships, rampant materialism, social and global economic injustice, sexism and racism. I have been part of Christian groups, both high level consultations and church Bible studies, where it is easy to point the finger at 'the world'. But we need to see our own responsibility.

John Stott puts the blame directly at the Church's door: 'When any community deteriorates, the blame should be attached where it belongs: not to the community which is going bad, but to the church which is failing in its responsibility as salt to stop it going bad.'[2]

Concerned Christians often feel helpless and overawed by the scale and speed of the changes in society. As a minister of a local church, I occasionally get members wanting me to preach sermons denouncing the evils of society. Church leaders at national and international level are often criticised for not speaking out more often on sin or social evils. The Church is encouraged to oppose betting shops, sex shops or Sunday trading. While all these things need to be addressed, this is not primarily what being salt of the earth is all about. On a purely practical level, sermons and national Church leaders have very little influence. The Bishop of Durham remarked recently that he got down from the pulpit after his first few sermons disappointed that the world had not been changed through them! I know the feeling.

However, if individual followers of Jesus act in their day by day lives, then things can change. For example, television producers take note if there are only a few hundred calls or letters after a programme. One person standing up in an office situation for what is right can change the whole atmosphere.

A second obvious thing about salt is that it gives a taste to something that is bland. Christian faith gives a taste to life, and taste makes something more attractive and satisfying. Christians are meant to make life, culture, cities and nations attractive and satisfying for all people. In a difficult area of Liverpool one of our churches provides a Saturday morning Kidz Club for children. It is the highlight of the week for the 200 children who crowd in. The club itself and the weekly visits to the children by the leaders affects the whole community, changing the atmosphere of despair and violence to hope. It is about Christian holiness in action.

Salt is different in its taste, and so Christians are called to be different. I have often fallen into the trap of being different in an arrogant way, looking down on others. But Jesus was different and he made a difference. He challenges me to be salt in society by living without concern for prejudice, power or influence, and living as a servant, demonstrating compassion and standing for justice.

My other mistake has been to doubt whether this is possible or whether the attempt to live a holy life will actually achieve anything. When I look at some of the problems of a city like Liverpool where we have lived for eight years, can anything be done? Yet the thing about salt is that just a little can affect a great mass. (I always need to remember that when cooking!) Individuals such as Shaftesbury in the area of child labour and William Wilberforce in the area of slavery, exercised huge influence in correcting injustice and dismantling evil structures. John Wesley in the eighteenth century, through his preaching and banding Christians together in small groups, had a profound effect on the nation, so much so that some claim that he saved England from revolution.

To be a holy person in the world is not to be negative and judgemental, but through love to bring a difference to where you are. Have you ever been with friends when a racial joke is told? How can we be holy in that situation? How can we be salt?

However, perhaps the most important thing about salt is that it needs to be spread to do any good. I remember skidding down an icy road while seeing a large pile of salt by the roadside – no one had actually spread the salt. If salt is going to be effective, it needs to be in the places where it can make a difference.

It is so easy for Christians to turn into piles of salt by the roadside. Jenny came to university as a new Christian. She was so thrilled with her new faith that she joined the Christian Union and many other Christian groups including our church. Halfway through her second year she suddenly realised what had happened. She had no friends at university who were not Christians. She lived with other Christians in a house, she ate lunches with Christians, and she even went to movies with

Christians. Where could she be salt of the earth? She had effectively become salt of the salt!

It is very easy to lose our balance in all of this. We lose friendships with those who are not Christians. The prayer meeting becomes more important than the union meeting or the basketball club. Some Christians feel so threatened by the world that they retreat into the haven of a Christian sub-culture.

To be salt in society is often like walking a· tightrope. A leading scientist who is a committed Christian is involved at the forefront of developments in genetic engineering. Some Christians have criticised him heavily, saying that Christians should not be involved in such an area as it is 'tampering in the realm of God'. The scientist replies that a proper biblical understanding does not mean that Christians should have nothing to do with genetics, and in addition if Christians are not involved then who is going to provide the ethical salt that will guard against the dangers of such developments? Often criticised by both Christians and those who are not, this scientist is responding to God's call to holy living.

Another friend works in television, not for a Christian broadcaster but on religious programmes for one of the major terrestrial channels. He is continually frustrated by the constraints on his work but he makes such a tremendous difference by being there. Kriss Akabusi, the British Olympic silver medallist in the 400m hurdles, and television presenter, once said, 'I believe that God is primarily calling me to be a witness where I am . . . rather than a celebrity Christian speaking at a different church each Sunday.'

Ben is a top musician and songwriter. At university he came to our church but found that because of being involved in shows and musicals he could not join all the activities of our student group. He felt that we judged him and viewed him as lacking commitment. That became part of a move away from the Christian faith. As he was led back to Christian faith he realised that God had called him to be a witness in areas that the rest of us could not be. He is rarely able to join us for Sunday worship as he is touring with professional shows and has to experience fellowship and worship in different ways. He is walking the holy tightrope.

After stating that his disciples are the salt of the earth, Jesus goes on to say a curious thing. He begins to talk about salt losing its saltiness (v13b). Now of course any chemist will tell us that sodium chloride does not lose its taste, salt is salt. Some biblical scholars patronisingly say that Jesus is being quaint but not knowing what he is talking about. However, the salt in use in Palestine in Jesus' time mainly came from the Dead Sea. It was contaminated with other minerals, and during storage the salt could be dissolved out of the mixture leaving the substance tasteless. It literally became good for nothing.

If Christians can withdraw into their own little world, then the opposite danger is that we can be so influenced by the world that we lose our distinctiveness. No longer do we promote good and oppose evil, and no longer do our lives bring taste to the society we live in. We all face the danger of losing our balance the other way, that is conforming to the world in such a way that we are no different.

How can we stay salty? Our salt comes from the life of Jesus within us, encouraged by our devotional relationship with him and the support of fellow Christians around us. This is a tight-rope. Too much fellowship or too little? It is a learning experience where we do make mistakes. We need to constantly look to Jesus to guide us and help us – to send us into situations where we need to be salt, and to check that we still make a difference.

2. The light of the world

The second image follows on from the first. 'You are the light of the world,' says Jesus (v14). The implication of this cannot be avoided. It implies that the world without the followers of Jesus is in darkness.

That would not be a universally acknowledged truth in the Western world today, or more particularly with the people I know who are not Christians. In Liverpool I work as chaplain at a large university where day by day I can see human achievements in science, technology, literature, art and philosophy. There is an overriding sense of Western society being 'enlightened' and having passed out of the dark ages.

However, the very things which show human achievements also remind me of the human problem. We take something good and mess it up. As we pass through the millennium it is difficult not to look back with deep despair, as well as thankfulness. The turn of the last century had a great deal of optimism. The emergence of technology, the belief that education would transform society for good, and the acceptance that wars would cease gave a confidence that was quickly shattered by two world wars, Hiroshima, Vietnam, apartheid, sexual exploitation of women and children, famine and the destruction of the environment.

James Cameron's film *Titanic* became the biggest movie of all time, with ticket sales of $600 million dollars in the US alone. I kept joking that I did not want to see it because I already knew the ending. When I did see it, it deeply affected me. Perhaps it was the contrasts. The power and pride in technology contrasted with its failure and frailty. The goodness of love and the selfishness of human beings. The hope that 'the heart will go on' and the finality and ugliness of death.

We cannot escape the darkness of this world or the darkness within each of us. Where will light come from? Jesus himself uses the expression 'I am the light of the world' (Jn 8:12). He is the true light in the darkness. Through his life, death and resurrection he showed what God was really like and what the world could be like in relationship with him.

So how can we be the light of the world? At school we discovered that in one particular classroom the sun was just in the right position during a boring afternoon religious education lesson. With a careful positioning of our watches we could reflect light into the eyes of the teacher effectively blinding him to the rest of the classroom. It was fun at the time and of course I feel great shame about it now! But it only worked if the glass on the face of the watch was aligned exactly with the position of the sun. As we get our lives 'aligned' or in a right relationship with Jesus so we become the (reflected) light of the world.

Jesus says that this role is inevitable. Just as a city on a hill cannot be hidden, so the light of his followers will be clearly seen. Indeed, part of the very purpose of being a follower of Jesus is to give light. It would be silly to light a lamp and then put it under a bowl! What does it mean to be the light of the world in this way? Light exposes darkness. Cricket is a game that goes on for most of the day and needs good light to see the ball. Sitting at a match not so long ago, I did not notice how bad the light had become until I glanced over at the scoreboard. There the light of the score, insignificant in broad daylight, now twinkled out in the increasing darkness.

Holy Christians are called to expose the dark, to be real about sin and corruption and to stand for what is good. In a particular part of Liverpool, my colleagues in church leadership stand against drug-pushers and gang warfare, but at the same time have to stand against social deprivation and unjust police tactics against the community. They personally bear the cost of being light in the community.

Not only does light expose the dark, it also shows the way out of the dark. The 'light at the end of the tunnel' allows us to find our way out. Christians are called not just to condemn, or simply to show a better way, but to actively help others out of the dark.

Alan Redpath was one of the great Bible teachers of a previous generation. His sermons, printed in many books, emphasised the theme of holiness time and time again. He was pastor at the Moody Memorial Church in Chicago and then at Charlotte Baptist Church in Edinburgh. It was then that a cerebral stroke forced him to retire but he found an international role in speaking and teaching.

He often came to speak at our university Christian Union. I remember one evening in particular when, before he started to read the Bible passage, he said, 'Before I start, I just want to testify that my life was changed during your Annual General Meeting last year.' Now, I had never known anyone changed during an Annual General Meeting, never mind a world-famous preacher well on in years!

He went on to explain. He and his wife had been living in the grounds of a lovely Bible school and life was great. The previous year he had come to our Christian Union to speak but had found that before his talk was the short annual meeting with reports given by the officers. The President gave a report in which he made the observation that he felt many of today's students had lost the element of sacrifice in their Christian lives. Alan Redpath said that God had taken that word and pushed it deep into his heart and mind. He began to realise that life was very nice, but where was the sacrifice? He went home and prayed it over with his wife. Some months later they decided to move to Birmingham to a block of flats in order to witness to and serve others.

That is holy sacrifice. To make the sacrifice to be salt and light of the world. We need to ask whether we are where we are needed. At the same time, are we so involved in the world that we are no different from it?

Study and action

One book to read: R. Frost and D. Wilkinson, *A New Start? Hopes and Dreams for the New Millennium* (Hodder Headline: London, 1999).

One outline for discussion:

1. Is the church prayer meeting more or less important than joining the local sports or social club?

2. What things make us lose our saltiness as Christians?
3. Are there too many pressures on us in our church life? What are they?
4. How can we support one another to be salt and light?

Question for yourself: Which areas that you encounter in your day to day life most need salt and light?

One action to take: On a sheet of paper, list in some detail the activities of a typical week. With a highlighter pen mark in one colour where your time is spent with people the majority of whom are Christians. With a different colour mark where your time is spent with people the majority of whom are not Christians. Are you happy about the result? If not, what are you going to do?

Notes

1. D. M. Lloyd-Jones, *The sermon on the Mount* (IVP: Leicester, 1978), p. 153.
2. J. R. W. Stott, *The Message of the sermon on the Mount* (IVP: Leicester, 1978), p. 89.

4

HOLIER THAN THOU?

The meeting was going well. We were trying to put young volunteers into teams to serve churches in different parts of the country. I was taking a back seat and my mind was often elsewhere. We were almost finished when one name came up over which one of the leaders expressed some uncertainty. He said, 'When he prayed last night he lost the anointing. He just continued to pray without the Spirit's anointing and you could sense it immediately.' To be honest I did not have the slightest idea what he was talking about. I had heard the prayer but I could not sense anything immediately. I suppose I should have asked what he meant but I found myself in inner turmoil – if I ask, then will he doubt my spiritual 'qualifications' to be in this meeting? I tried to shrink into my chair and keep my head down.

However, the leader of the meeting turned to me. 'David, would you like to lead us in prayer on this?' The honest answer was 'no way', but I nodded in the good spiritual fashion that I thought was expected of me. My turmoil grew. Would I also pray without the Spirit's anointing and would all the others sense it immediately? I said a few words and lowered my voice a little to appear more spiritual. For the next couple of days every time any one of the leaders approached me I shuddered inside, worried that they had seen through my lack of spirituality!

I may have grown a little to a point where such situations do not worry me as much, but the area with which I have the most trouble in keeping my balance is with other Christians. I find myself swaying between feeling threatened by other people or looking down on other people. The problem is trying to judge 'my holiness' in relation to theirs. Those who make me feel threatened expose a deep insecurity and even shame that I am not more holy.

I look down on other Christians to give me a sense of self-achievement and to avoid feeling threatened. This is often the case with being a pastor or minister of a church. I am well aware of my own failings and the weakness of the church where I minister. Sometimes I go to other churches and find myself relieved if they are not as 'good' as ours, or find myself critical if they do appear to be better.

The American writer Richard Lovelace has said that one person's piety is another person's poison. I know exactly what he means. How are you to be holy with other people around, and in particular with other Christians around?

If holiness is defined as separation, then many people view holiness as a very individualistic pursuit. Indeed, it is tempting to do this. This view surfaced in the fourth century, in the extreme form of Simeon Stylites, who lived on top of a pillar for thirty years! I sometimes find myself wanting to be holy alone. Because of my insecurity I find it difficult to share my inner feelings, doubts and struggles with others. I fear what other people may think of me and so I am nervous of how they view me.

In fact, many of these feelings are reinforced by an increasing view that sees spirituality as a very solo journey. New Age thinking often emphasises the importance of inner experience and indeed some Christians exalt inner experience above everything else. We fall into the trap of talking about 'my worship', as if the only person present at church on a Sunday morning is God. I can easily convince myself that as long as I get my morning quiet time in, then holiness will inevitably follow – and I need not admit to anyone just how bad I am at praying in the morning.

In addition, the Christian Church has the habit of worrying about how one person's lack of holiness may affect the rest. I had been asked to lead a Bible teaching day at a particular church and had been invited with my family to stay on for a few days' holiday in a hotel owned by one of the church members. It was going to be a real treat. However, a few weeks after accepting the invitation, a letter came from the church secretary which said, 'After studying your books and having debated them at our recent church council meeting, we are sorry but we must withdraw the invitation.' I was considered unsound and even dangerous. My views on creation would pollute the faithful believers. I was sad and amused, not least at the image of my books being debated at a church council meeting!

This isolationist view of holiness is expressed in many ways. Some churches will have nothing to do with other churches whom they judge to be less sound than they are. Even within churches, small groups can become separate from other members of the same church. They view themselves as more spiritual than others. I spoke at a student Christian group recently who later told me that they had formed because the other evangelical student group had 'lost the vision'.

Do you have to cut yourself off from everyone else to be holy? I certainly believe that truth is important but I do not believe that the Bible sees holiness as requiring separation. We fall into the trap of seeing Christian faith in an individualistic way, and holiness as something we achieve. That is why I find the following passage so helpful. It expresses one of the major doctrines of Scripture, that is the relationship of holiness to other members of God's holy people.

[17]So I tell you this, and insist on it in the Lord, that you must no longer live as the Gentiles do, in the futility of their thinking. [18]They are darkened in their understanding and separated from the life of God because of the ignorance that is in them due to the hardening of their hearts. [19]Having lost all sensitivity, they have given themselves over to sensuality so as to indulge in every kind of impurity, with a continual lust for more.

[20]You, however, did not come to know Christ that way. [21]Surely you heard of him and were taught in him in accordance with the truth that is in Jesus. [22]You were taught, with regard to your former way of life, to put off your old self, which is being corrupted by its deceitful desires; [23]to be made new in the attitude of your minds: [24]and to put on the new self, created to be like God in true righteousness and holiness.

[25]Therefore each of you must put off falsehood and speak truthfully to your neighbour, for we are all members of one body. [26]'In your anger do not sin': Do not let the sun go down while you are still angry, [27]and do not give the devil a foothold. [28]Those who have been stealing must steal no longer, but must work, doing something useful with their own hands, that they may have something to share with those in need.

[29]Do not let any unwholesome talk come out of your mouths, but only what is helpful for building others up according to their needs, that it may benefit those who listen. [30]And do not grieve the Holy Spirit of God, with whom you were sealed for the day of redemption. [31]Get rid of all bitterness, rage and anger, brawling and slander, along with every form of malice. [32]Be kind and compassionate to one another, forgiving each other, just as in Christ God forgave you.

5 Be imitators of God, therefore, as dearly loved children [2]and live a life of love, just as Christ loved us and gave himself up for us as a fragrant offering and sacrifice to God.

(Ephesians 4:17–5:2)

Paul's letter to the Ephesians is one of the richest letters in the New Testament. He overflows with excitement and praise for what God has done for us in Christ and wants the Ephesian

Christians to understand this and share his praise (Eph 1:1 – 2:10). However, part of this work is not only about a new relationship of the individual with God, it is also about our relationships with one another (eg Eph 2:19: 4:1–16). It is these two themes, what God has done and the corporate consequences, that Paul now details in the context of holiness.

1. The capacity to be holy is a gift

What is life like 'separated from God' (Eph 4:18)? Paul explains that people separated from God are:

- darkened in their understanding (v18)
- ignorant (v18)
- have no sensitivity (v19)
- indulgent (v19)
- continually lusting for more (v19)

It is a painful picture of people with no purpose, no understanding and no control in life. Of course there are many who are not Christians who do not fit this picture, and we must quickly say there are many who call themselves Christians who do fit this picture!

Paul is not describing an individual, but stating broad characteristics of what life without God ultimately is about. His purpose is not to condemn those who are not Christians, but to say to those who are Christians that this is what you would be if God had not done something for you.

'You, however' (v20) introduces the contrast that Paul draws. In fact, something has happened to those who follow Jesus. Paul describes this discipleship as knowing Christ, hearing of him, and being taught in him. This is not just an emotional response but a realisation that the truth is in Jesus.

In this a change has come about (vv 22–24). The implication of this change is that the old self is to be put off, and the new self is to be put on. The tense used in the Greek is the aorist.

This tense means one act in the past with lasting consequences. The old self is corrupt, rotten and perishing but the
new self is the new creation in the image of God in true righteousness and holiness. In Greek there are two words for new,
kainos which means fresh and *neos* which means young. Paul
uses both here to bring out the full implications of what God
has done and what is expected of us. He expects Christians 'to
be made new in the attitude of your minds' (v23). The word
here is *neos* and it is in the present tense. It suggests the constant rejuvenation of the mind. We would use the sense of the
word in terms of greeting someone as, 'you're looking a new
person after your holiday!' They have been renewed.

However, this constant renewal of the mind is only possible
because God has done something very fundamental for us. He
has created a 'new self' (v24). The word here is *kainos* and
speaks of a new fresh creation. When our children play with
felt-tips, eat yoghurt or play in the garden, there are two ways
to deal with the ensuing dirty clothes. One way is to sponge
them while still on the children. However, sometimes they are
so dirty and spoiled that only buying new clothes will do! Even
then the new clothes need to be constantly washed.

Holiness comes from both these things. There is the decisive
act of putting off the old self and putting on the new, 'bought'
for us in the death of Jesus, and there is the continuous
renewal of the mind by the truth of Jesus.

How is holiness possible? Where does the new self come
from? Where does the truth of Jesus come from? Simply the
gift of God. We don't make the garment, we don't think up
the new idea that renews our mind, we receive.

The consequence of this cuts away any type of pride. I am
still learning this, but it gives tremendous freedom. Bishop
Festo Kivengere once said, 'At the foot of the cross is level
ground.' I have no right to look down on other people and
indeed I do not have to. My own growth in holiness is not my
own achievement, it is a gift from God. My security is not to

be found by comparing myself with other people, it is to be found in trusting what God has already done and what he promises for the future. As I have begun to learn and experience this so my relationships with other Christians have become deeper and more real.

2. The consequences of holiness are corporate

The word 'therefore' (v25) introduces Paul's application of this doctrine that holiness is a gift. He is saying that on the basis of this understanding, this consequence follows. Let your behaviour be consistent with the person you are. What is perhaps surprising is that such an amazing insight to the nature of holiness is not worked out in terms of spiritual devotion but in very practical instructions concerning relationships in the local church.

a) Tell the truth (v25)

We are members of one body: so, then, do not tell lies to one another. Perhaps we underestimate the force of this.

A principal of a Bible college was once telling me of the type of thing that can happen in such a pressure-cooker environment with so many Christians living and working together, and wanting to look good in front of one another. On one particular night of the week the college would gather and people would be invited to share what God had done in their lives. During this time a new student got up and began the most amazing story of how he had become a Christian. It was an X-rated story of sex, drugs and a time in a prison. In fact there was so much of it that the meeting had to finish and the student was told he could continue the following week.

However, during the week there was a knock on the principal's door. In came the student with an older student. The student, it turned out, had made up all of his story, and had been found out by the older student who had actually been in the prison that had been referred to. The principal asked the student why he had made up the testimony. His reply was that he thought his real testimony was too boring, but he had found that as he added 'more spice' then more people would listen to him.

We all want to impress. We might not think that we tell out-right lies, but we do mislead one another. We project images to other people to make us look good. I have often gone to church really struggling and yet when someone asks me how I am, I reply, 'Fine'! I know that when I say good-bye to people at the end of a service, the standard remark of, 'Thank you for a lovely service' can mask anger, doubt or boredom!

We need to be truthful with one another. If we are to be the 'members of one body' we can only grow together if we are real and honest with one another. If I am to be holy, I can only do it in relationship with other Christians. It is only as I have opened myself up to other Christians that I have found love, support and encouragement.

I hate to admit that I find things difficult or that I have too much to do. For the past few years a support group has helped me to share these things and at the same time I have been able to hear truth from them. This has liberated me in the work I do. It need not be a formal group. One or two Christian friends can share together and speak truth to one another.

The desire to speak truth to one another can also help us to be faithful to the Bible. I love it as a preacher when someone disagrees with me and is prepared to talk to me about it. I can find it hard to begin with, depending on how angry they are, but the conversation inevitably leads me to a deeper understanding.

Of course we need to be sensitive in the speaking of truth. Some eager Christian brothers and sisters use this verse as an excuse to 'tell the truth in love' to everyone regardless of time and place. A young preacher preaching their first sermon does not need to be told all of the things that need to be improved.

We often make the mistake of telling discouraging truth more than encouraging truth. When I first began leading a large prayer meeting, one older Christian would come to me every week and pick out one thing I had done well. I made a great many mistakes but that one word of encouragement did more for me than a rehearsal of my failures.

b) Be careful in your anger (v26)

It is not wrong to be angry, and as we shall see in a later chapter that part of being holy is to be angry. However, here Paul warns about the danger of anger. For anger can quickly turn into bitterness against a particular person. Such bitterness can pollute not only the Christian fellowship. The person who is bitter can become trapped within it.

In a large church there are always people who are members of the church, but no longer come. This may be for many reasons. I try to visit and see whether the people can come back. One of the saddest visits that I made was to a couple who had not been to church for years but before they left were at the heart of church life. They were lovely people and it was clear that their Christian faith meant much to them. I asked why they no longer came to church, wondering whether it was my preaching or the new styles of worship that had turned them away. The reason was bitterness. Another person in the church some ten years ago had made a comment which he thought was a joke but was not received by the couple as a joke. They literally left immediately. Their anger and hurt had turned into bitterness. This had stopped them coming to church and acted as a kind of spiritual cancer draining their spiritual life.

I say that I would never react to that extreme, but there have been many times in church life where people have hurt me and the anger has been allowed to turn into bitterness which messes up my life and indeed my relationships with others. If I am to be holy, then I need those relationships, for it is through them that the Holy Spirit encourages me and renews my mind.

Paul is very practical. Realising that in the church we do hurt one another, he gives us a good rule of thumb: Do not let the sun go down on your anger. That is, if someone makes you angry, talk about it with them quickly, the same day if possible. The longer you leave it, the more of a foothold you give to the devil. A friend of mine who is a Methodist minister would often bake a cake and take it around to anybody he thought he had offended or was angry with! It limited anger beautifully. So often our motive for anger can be wounded pride, and we need to act quickly to receive and give forgiveness if that is the case. If I attempted to bake a cake that might compound the difficulty, but a telephone call, a letter or a visit is just as good!

c) Work faithfully (v28)

Being holy has very practical consequences. We can easily see them as always negatives but Paul stresses the positives. It is not just that for Christians there should be no more stealing, but the positive is that we should work hard. The word he uses signifies strenuous toil which produces fatigue.

At the end of services at our church, people are engaged in all kinds of activity. Some are praying either by themselves or with people who request ministry. Others are in theological discussion with the preacher or with others. Others are neither praying or discussing. Some are putting the chairs away. Some are washing up the cups and saucers. Some are counting the offering and putting it in the safe. Which people are the most holy? Of course there is no distinction. To pray and work are both parts of the holy life and we need to value both.

Paul wants the church to be a place where we work for one another, sharing our gifts, time and energy with those in need. Such work needs to be honest. How many of us have done the menial task in order to look 'humble' in front of someone we want to impress? Work honestly, says Paul and to that we shall return in Chapter 9

d) Speak wisely (v29)

Our relationships are built on what we say to one another. 'Unwholesome' talk is rotten and worthless, affecting the whole atmosphere of church life. Paul encourages 'good' or 'helpful' talk or, as J. B. Phillips puts it, talk 'suitable for the occasion'.

Once again it is not just to stop swearing, although that is expected. Unwholesome talk can often be gossip. The justification of 'I'm just sharing this with you so that you can pray about it' can be used to share slander and lies. The effect of this can be catastrophic for a Christian community. I spent a day preaching at a church where I was given lunch by one group of people, tea by another and supper by yet another. All told me in 'concerned detail' stories about the other groups. Although a large church with a good reputation, the worship was dead – no doubt because of the gossip and breaking of relationships.

The positive aspect of this is to ask whether my words are helpful to others. Paul insists that we do not grieve the Holy Spirit through bitterness, rage and anger, brawling (the word is really self-assertion, so that everyone hears my grievance), slander or malice. Instead, be kind and compassionate and forgive each other.

A good test of how far we are progressing as holy people is how we speak to others. Those of us who are preachers or leaders need to remember that what we speak publicly needs to be backed up by how we speak privately. The greatest sermon in the world cannot hide the sin of gossip, envy and humiliating others by what we say. Indeed, in local church life problem after problem can be caused to unity and mission by people who do not speak wisely.

Therefore holiness is not something we accomplish by

ourselves or follow by ourselves. It is a joint activity with God and with other people. Such themes have sometimes been neglected in the popular view of holiness, but have always been there in those who reflect the biblical message. In the classic book *Holiness*, first published in 1879, J. C. Ryle comments:

> Sensational and exciting addresses by strange preachers or by women, loud singing, hot rooms, the constant sight of semi-religious feeling in the faces of all around you for several days, late hours, long protracted meetings, public profession of experience – all this . . . is very interesting at the time . . . (but) do those who attend these meetings become more holy, meek, unselfish, kind, self-denying and Christ-like at home? Do they become more content with their position in life and more free from restless craving . . . do fathers, mothers, husbands and other relatives and friends find them more pleasant and easy to live with?[1]

Those are questions we can ask of ourselves if we want to walk the holy tightrope.

Study and action

One book to read: R. Warner, *21st Century Church* (Kingsway: Eastbourne, 1999).

One outline for discussion:
1. How can your local fellowship encourage holy relationships within its own body?
2. What are the practical consequences of seeing holiness as a gift?
3. How do you deal with anger at other Christians?
4. How can you discourage gossip in your local fellowship?

One question for yourself: Is there anybody that you are ready to forgive or from whom you need to ask for forgiveness?

One action to take: Go and see that person or write or telephone – now!

Notes

1. J. C. Ryle, *Holiness* (Evangelical Press: Herts, 1979), pp. xiii–xiv.

5

THE GRUBBINESS OF HOLINESS

In the movie *Indecent Proposal*, Robert Redford offers one million dollars for one night with Demi Moore. The film traces such a proposal and its effect on Moore and husband Woody Harrelson. It is a very clever plot. The point it raises is fundamental. How much is a person worth? And what is love worth?

At one level there is a very easy answer to the question of the worth of a human being. Someone once wrote that a person was 'nothing but iron enough for one medium-sized nail, sugar enough to fill seven cups of tea, lime enough to whitewash one chicken coop, phosphorus enough to tip 2,200 matches, magnesium enough for one dose of salts, fat enough for seven bars of soap, potash to explode one toy crane, and sulphur to rid one dog of fleas'. At current market prices that comes out at about 54p!

This perhaps does not build up any sense of self-worth! Yet in many more serious ways, there are various attitudes in our society which say very much the same thing. Mary had left school and college with good qualifications and had risen quickly to a post of responsibility in the Health Service. However, she began to be stalked by a man, lost confidence and had to give up her job. She spent a great deal of her time looking after her husband and children but then her husband left her and she had a series of serious car accidents. Battling with great courage through these things she still had to face many negative attitudes. Employers did not want her – they would not explicitly say that she was too old and too disabled but she got that impression. Some condemned her for making a mess of her life, even though she was a victim. The church found it hard to provide support to a single person. The effect of all of this was that her own self-worth was continually eroded until she began to believe that her life had no value at all.

Mary is not alone. To some, if you fail exams then you are worthless. If you are unemployed, if your skin is the wrong colour, if you come from the wrong part of town, if you are too young, if you are too old, if you are female, if you are disabled, or if you have made a mess of your life, then there are many voices to tell you that you are worthless. Those voices are not just outside the church but in it as well.

Often, our Western attitudes see the value or worth of a person in terms of the power they have over others, or the things they have achieved. I went to a church to preach where I was not personally known. Not wanting to make a fuss I sat down in the congregation. No one spoke or welcomed me. In fact I got the distinct impression that I was sitting in someone's seat. However, after I had been introduced and had preached, people were falling over themselves to welcome me. One person said, 'If we had known who you were we would have welcomed you properly!' I was valued just because I was the preacher rather than being valued as a human being.

These attitudes lead to a doubting of our self-worth and the reaction of selfishness to try and grab attention. Madonna, speaking of her obsessive need to succeed, said that it came from losing the care of her parents. 'You overcompensate and become an attention getter.' Richard Gere commented once, 'I don't think anyone starts doing creative work because they are serving humanity. They want to get laid, they want to get money and they want to get attention.'

In order to establish our own value, we grab attention, we use others and we put each other down. But it need not be like that. As I have encountered the care of the holy God I have been given the security of the knowledge that I am loved and valued. That is true not just for me, but also for Mary and for many others. That in itself becomes the motive to show holy care to others and give to them a sense of love and value.

When we think of the holiness of God we think about how different God is, that is, how morally pure, how separated from this awful world he is. As I have thought about his holiness then I have sometimes questioned my own value. If we are so different from God are we worth anything at all? In the following psalm the writer asks just that sort of question. But the answer is very different.

[1]O Lord, our Lord,
How majestic is your name in all the earth!
You have set your glory above the heavens.
[2]From the lips of children and infants you have ordained praise
because of your enemies, to silence the foe and the avenger.
[3]When I consider your heavens,
the work of your fingers,
the moon and the stars,
which you have set in place,
[4]what are mere mortals that you are mindful of them,
human beings that you care for them?
[5]You made them a little lower than the heavenly beings
and crowned them with glory and honour.
[6]You made them rulers over the works of your hands;
you put everything under their feet:
[7]all flocks and herds,
and the beasts of the field,
[8]the birds of the air,
and the fish of the sea,

all that swim the paths of the seas.
⁹O Lord, our Lord,
how majestic is your name in all the earth!

(Psalm 8)

1. A God of holy care

As an astrophysicist I was used to big numbers. I knew that our
sun is one of one hundred billion stars in the Milky Way
galaxy. The Milky Way is one of billions of galaxies in the universe. I had said to other people that there were more stars in
the universe than grains of sand on the beaches of the world.
But on one evening in Pune in India it took on more
significance.

I was there as a young scientist working and teaching in
Bombay. I had travelled up into the hills to Pune to give a
lecture at the physics department. I felt a long way from home,
there was no one there that I knew and for the past few weeks I
had not met a Christian or been able to find a local church to
worship in.

I sat looking up at the stars, seeing them shining brightly
without the hindrance of British street lights. I suddenly felt
small, insignificant and alone. I was the product of the ashes
of a dead supernova remnant, in an obscure part of an
average spiral galaxy. The old Police song 'Message in a Bottle'
came into my mind. I did feel just a castaway, an island lost at
sea!

I was not filled with awe, I was filled with despair. Any God
who created this universe must be so great and how could this
God really be interested in me? Even if he was interested then
surely he would look at my sinfulness and in his perfection be
revolted. I had been a Christian for a number of years but I
don't think I had really sensed God's holiness in this kind of
depth before.

I went back to my room. There was no television to take my

mind away to other things, and no fellow Christians to give me reassurance. There was just me and God and some very large mosquitoes!

I guess that if I was a really spiritual person then I would have opened my Bible straight away. It took me some time before I did and I turned to Psalm 8. I knew the psalm a little, but as I read it seemed it had been written just for me.

The psalm begins with an affirmation of God's greatness and worth. In encountering God, as we have seen already, there is an overwhelming sense of his holiness and majesty. That night in Pune it almost terrified me. But as I read on, the psalmist asks the question, 'what are mere mortals that you are mindful of them, human beings that you care for them?' (v4). The answer hit me with real force, 'You made them a little lower than the heavenly beings and crowned them with glory and honour' (v5). In contrast to finding self-worth in what you are, or the power or achievements you possess, this psalm says fundamentally that *self-worth comes from relationship*. In fact the supreme relationship of God's love for me.

My despair began to turn into excitement. He is not simply a God divorced from the world. This holy God, creator of the billions of stars, cares for me. I began to remember some of the stories of the New Testament. It is the care which underlies the ministry of Jesus. So that when a leper, shunned not only because of fear of disease but also ritual uncleanliness comes to Jesus, Jesus reaches out and touches him. For Jesus is 'filled with compassion' (Mk 1:40–45). When the Pharisees and the Herodians set up a trap for Jesus with a man with a withered hand, Jesus cares so much that he heals him on the Sabbath (Mk 3:1–6). When a woman simply touches Jesus for healing, Jesus is concerned for that woman as an individual (Mk 5:21–43). Throughout the Gospels, time after time Jesus demonstrates personal care for those around him.

Then I remembered the cross. As Jesus faced death in the garden of Gethsemane he cared enough not to turn back. As he was whipped, mocked, spat at, and crowned with tangled thorns, he cared enough to go on loving. As he was nailed to a cross and experienced total alienation from his Father, as he bore in himself all the consequences of our sin, he cared enough to say, 'Father, forgive them, they do not know what they are doing.'

That is holy care. It is quite different from our normal image of care. It is total self-giving love shown in costly·action. It is a demonstration of the grubbiness of holiness, for it is about the holy God who empties himself to live among us and eventually die our death in the pain and blood of the cross.

That night in Pune reminded me again of what it cost a holy God to care for me. It gave me an inner sense of worth, peace and joy. In my mosquito net I sang and praised God. It is an experience which has been repeated time after time, either in my own experience or in the experience of others.

Neil was articulate and intelligent, but his life had been a journey from institution to borstal to prison to sleeping rough. Over a cup of coffee I had been speaking about the value of the church I attended, when he said, 'You know you have all these people either in your family or in your church who care for you. In fact, from what you have been saying some would even die for you. But I have no one.' I did not know what to say. Finally, the only thing I could say was, 'Neil, I do know someone who cares for you. In fact, he cares so much that he has died for you.' Many months later, in another part of the country, Neil came to experience that care and love of Jesus, and it transformed his life.

It also came powerfully to me in a small Methodist church in Rio. The service was in Portuguese and I could not understand a word. The congregation was poor but full of joy. The only musical instrument they had was a set of drums yet the singing was some of the most inspiring I had ever heard. One song in particular intrigued me. During the song people would point at one another. To be pointed at with words you cannot understand is quite unnerving! After the service I asked what the song was about. As people were pointing they were singing, 'You are special and loved because you are created by God.' Here in a society which devalued these poor people, the love of God was giving people self-worth, hope and security.

No matter who you are, where you come from, whatever you have done or not done in the past, God cares for you. The world may say you are worthless, but God says that you are not.

2. A people of holy care

The writer now goes on to remind humanity not only of God's care but our own responsibility to care. Verse 6 reflects imagery from Genesis 1, 'You have made them rulers over the works of your hands, you have put all things under their feet.' God's care for us leads to a commission to care. Made in the image of God, being given the responsibility under him for the works of his hands, does not mean that we lord it over the rest of God's creation. It means that we reflect God's image in caring for others and the physical world. We are called to be stewards whose stewardship is exercised as servants.

The pressures of our society often convince us that the way to be fully human is to use other people, to be selfish and look after our own interests. However, there is part of us which always admires the person who cares. At the height of popularity of the boy band Take That, the members had the world (and most of its female population) at their feet. Yet when Jason Orange was asked in an interview what he was looking for in a girl, he said, 'Being caring and kind are the main two things for me. Someone who is concerned about others is the biggest turn on for me.' Not the greatest piece of moral philosophy, but he was saying something about seeing the best in human beings when they are caring for others. We are the people we were created to be when we care.

The reason that many of us do not care, is that we do not fully know that we are cared for. It is often that we have such incredibly low self-esteem that leads to an uncaring attitude to others. The source of our selfishness comes from not knowing the love of God, and not being the people we are meant to be.

The love of God is so important, especially when we recognise that caring costs. One Australian soap is characterised by the immortal lines: 'Neighbours, everybody needs good neighbours, just a friendly word each morning helps to make a better day. Neighbours, should be there for one another, that's when good neighbours become good friends.' It's just a little too sickly sweet, especially if your neighbour does not offer a 'friendly word'! The real world is a world where neighbours are not sun-bronzed, blond-haired actors but are often difficult people to like, never mind love. In the title of another TV series, they are 'neighbours from hell'.

That's why when Jesus is asked about neighbour love he tells a story of a man lying broken and bloody by the side of a road (Lk 10:25–37). The ones reputed for their holiness, the priest and the Levite, pass by on the other side of the road. Perhaps they were afraid of polluting their holy life or they simply could not be bothered. The Jewish audience probably felt they knew what would happen next. Jesus would say, 'And then a Jewish lay person came by and took care of the man.' After all, the audience would know well such anti-clerical stories.

Yet Jesus takes the story in a totally different direction. It is a Samaritan who takes the costly step of crossing the cultural divide by caring for him, and who binds his wounds and pays for his care. It is this Samaritan, hated by the Jews, who shows what neighbour love is all about.

God's care is costly. The writer of the letter to the Hebrews uses the imagery of Psalm 8 to speak about Jesus. He writes, 'But we see Jesus, who was made a little lower than the angels, now crowned with glory and honour' (Heb 2:9). But the verse does not end there. It continues, 'crowned with glory and honour because he suffered death, so that by the grace of God he might taste death for everyone'. The care of God is seen supremely in the costly sacrifice on the cross.

Many times I have been the priest or the Levite. It has been easy to try and rationalise my lack of care. My neighbour may need a lift to the supermarket but I have too much to do already. I am worried about that situation where people have fallen out but if I try to help I will only complicate things. What can I do? Other people are better placed and gifted to help than me. Each of these excuses my have some truth to them but they are often used simply to avoid the cost of caring.

To care is to give of oneself in a costly way. A Christian friend of mine lived next door to someone who arrived back drunk most nights. My friend would often have to help this man to bed, take his contact lenses out, clear up his vomit, and make sure that he would not choke during the night. After many nights, the man said to him, 'Why do you do this?' My friend replied, 'Because I care for you.' The man said, 'Why do you care?' My friend replied, 'Because God cares.' That is the grubbiness of holy caring.

We are created to be holy carers. In Jesus we see the supreme demonstration of God's care for us, and the supreme example of what our care should be like. In the cost of caring we have a holy God who walks with us, giving us strength for the task. Sometimes, an obsession for our own inward purity can stop us seeing the needs of the smelly old bloke who lives down our street. Or the person in our class that no one else talks to. Or the ordinary person whose needs do not stick out, but nevertheless is loved and cared for by God.

An old parable is told of a man who fell into a deep pit and couldn't get out. A subjective person came along and said, 'I feel for you down there.' An objective person came along and said, 'It's logical that someone would fall down there.' A religious person came along and said, 'Only bad people fall into pits.' A realist said, 'That's a pit.' A physicist calculated the force necessary to get him out of the pit. A tax collector asked him if he was paying taxes on the pit. A council inspector asked him if he had a permit to dig the pit. An evasive person came along and avoided the subject of the pit altogether. A self-pitying person said, 'You haven't seen anything until you've seen my pit.' Jesus, seeing the man, took him by the hand and lifted him out of the pit.

Study and action

One book to read: J. White, *God's Pursuing Love* (Eagle, 1998).

One outline for discussion:
1. What does it mean to be 'crowned with glory and honour'?
2. Have there been moments when you have seen the greatness of God in creation?
3. How do those moments make you feel?
4. How can you encourage and support those in your local fellowship to care for others?

One question for yourself: Who needs you as a neighbour?

One action to take: Do something for someone who needs to feel valued – invite them for a meal, send them a card, or buy them a present.

PART TWO
Holiness and the Individual

6

HOLY SEX

The average twenty-four-year-old British woman has slept with eleven men, goes to bed with a new man either on a first date or within a fortnight, and wants sex at least three times a night. At least that was the reported conclusion of a survey for *FHM* magazine of 2000 women. The tabloid press greeted this conclusion with stories about sex-mad British women, at the same time demonstrating themselves their obsession with sex and the need to reinforce male fantasies.

We live in a culture which speaks openly about sex. Sex is portrayed and talked about everywhere. Explicit stories and pictures used to be sold only to men in back alley sex shops. They are now freely available through newsagents, terrestrial and cable television, videos, feature films and the Internet.

In the past few decades we have had a sexual revolution perhaps as great as the 1960s. British soap operas such as *Eastenders* or *Coronation Street,* shown well before the 9pm watershed, feature stories on impotence, gay relationships and transsexuals as well as the usual adultery. One of the fastest growing sections of the magazine trade in recent years has been for men with magazines such as *Loaded, Esquire* and *FHM.* The 'new laddism' of such magazines still feature naked women but also provide articles on 'How to stimulate her clitoris'. It is a demonstration of how the revolution has many paradoxes, not least that women are still exploited but are also asserting their sexuality. Men have been forced to respond to that.

For women the revolution has been even greater. For so long the passive victims of men's sexuality, women have taken more control of sex, although it has to be said they are still victims of violence, abuse and rape. The American feminist writer Camille Paglia points to Madonna as a symbol of the modern woman's understanding of sexuality – in control and loving it. The US television series, *Sex in the City*, starring Sarah Jessica Parker, was advertised in Britain under the caption 'These are the new generals of sex' showing four of the female stars.

Alongside their male counterparts, women's magazines such as *Cosmopolitan* , *Marie Claire* and *Elle* inevitably have at least one major article on sex, with the emphasis no longer on how to please a man but on how you can be in control of your orgasm. For teenagers and indeed for children sexuality is all around through the medium of the pop world, and teenage magazines. The British feminist writer Germaine Greer has recently lamented the fact that these magazines are full of advice on how to give your boyfriend oral sex, rather than the development of traditional hobbies. A recent copy of the magazine *19,* which is read by girls much younger than 19, has articles entitled 'For true relationship bliss, a girl's gotta take control of her sex life', and gives detailed advice on erogenous zones and how to get your partner to use them.

If there is open discussion of sex, it might not always be honest discussion. Articles on sex in the male magazines are not simply there to inform but to stimulate. It is interesting to contrast the *FHM* survey on the 'average woman' with the larger *Sexual Behaviour in Britain* survey carried out on 20,000 women. That survey showed that the majority of women in their twenties only had one or two sexual partners. The *FHM* survey was presented not just as public information but to stimulate men's fantasies that most women are sex mad. Beyond

this, images of sex are not used only to stimulate but to manipulate through advertising and selling. In a recent survey, the
advert for Diet Coke featuring a semi-naked window cleaner
was voted most popular advert, closely followed by a car advert
featuring a fully naked supermodel.

Christians are not immune from such influences. To live a life
without the mention of sex would involve cutting oneself off from
the vast majority of contemporary culture in television, film, art,
literature and magazines. Some Christians would argue that this
is the only way. However, is this really the way of holiness?

For the past few years at our church we have had a regular
series of evening services on contemporary issues and the
Christian faith. Often we have asked the congregation, made up
of teenagers, students and people in their twenties and thirties
what they would like in terms of topics. Each time, questions
about sex are inevitably top of the list, and the services seem to
attract the highest number. During the services themselves, we
have had an opportunity for people to write down questions
anonymously for us together to try and apply the Bible to this
area. The questions below are typical of the kind of issues
which face not only teenagers but many more people.

- Is masturbation sin?
- Should Christians go out with non-Christians?
- What's wrong with two people sleeping together if they are not
  married, as long as they are committed to each other?
- Can you be a Christian and in a homosexual relationship?

In fact there are many more questions deep below the surface
of these 'public' questions. There are those who are survivors of
abuse as children or adults. There are those longing for intimacy with another person but not finding it. There are those
who feel guilty at things they have thought and done and are
looking for forgiveness. There are those who think sex is 'dirty'
in some way.

We cannot ignore these questions, or expect Christians to live in a world cocooned from the everyday images and choices that are part of Western society. We may bemoan the fact that our society should be more holy, but that will only happen if Christians live out a view of sexuality which is holy.

It has always struck me just how positive the Bible is about sex. As a teenager my impression was always that the Bible was full of 'thou shalt nots'. But as I have tried to bring my own sexuality under the Bible's authority, then I see the dangers of its abuse but I also see its God-given goodness. Look, for example, at the following passage from Genesis:

[18]The Lord God said, 'It is not good for the man to be alone. I will make a helper suitable for him.'
[19]Now the Lord God had formed out of the ground all the beasts of the field and all the birds of the air. He brought them to the man to see what he would name them; and whatever the man called each living creature, that was its name. [20]So the man gave names to all the livestock, the birds of the air and all the beasts of the field. But for Adam no suitable helper was found. [21]So the Lord God caused the man to fall into a deep sleep; and while he was sleeping, he took one of the man's ribs and closed up the place with flesh.
[22]Then the Lord God made a woman from the rib he had taken out of the man, and he brought her to the man.
[23]The man said,

'This is now bone of my bones
and flesh of my flesh;
she shall be called "woman",
for she was taken out of man.'

[24]For this reason a man will leave his father and mother and be united to his wife, and they will become one flesh.[25] The man and his wife were both naked, and they felt no shame.

(Genesis 2:18–25)

1. Sex is good

Where does our understanding of sexuality come from? It may come from lots of sources. It may come from peer pressure and furtive conversations at school, parents, teaching from authority whether it be from school or church, experiences of abuse, media dreams and pictures, what we dream about for the future, pornography, or sexual experiences and experimentation. Some of these will be positive about sex, others will be very negative. As we try to understand ourselves or search for love, we can experience joy and excitement, or fear, guilt, anger and addiction.

Holy sex bases its understanding of sex on the fact that God created it for good. God created men and women and he created sex. The account of that creation in Genesis 2 amplifies the creating of male and female referred to in Genesis 1:27. It shows God taking the initiative in creating something that is good. God says that it is not good to be alone (2:18) and so part of man's flesh is taken to make woman so that they can come together in one flesh (2:24). This is a beautiful picture of intimacy and togetherness in diversity.

Sex is not just union, it is a kind of reunion. The phrase 'becoming one flesh' has a graphic illustration in the act of sexual intercourse, but it is much more than that. It is the God-given capacity for deep intimacy of body, mind and spirit.

Our sexuality is to be enjoyed. Indeed, later in the Old Testament, the Song of Songs is a celebration of such sexual enjoyment. In the past some Christians have found it too much and they have interpreted it as an allegory of the love of Christ for the Church. However, recent scholarship suggests that Song of Songs is a commentary on Genesis 2:24 and a manual on the blessing and reward of intimate married love. It is a kind of *Joy of Sex* or *Lovers' Guide* written by the Lord!

It is important to stress this because both experience and theology can undermine this. Some Christians will subtlety communicate that sex is somehow bad. Afraid of the abuse of sex they will constantly warn of its dangers, leaving teenagers with a deep-down belief that it is dirty and somehow not holy. I talked with one student who had been to a church which advocated the three-foot rule – that was how far you had to stay apart until you had been going out a few months. He said, 'It makes sex sound more dangerous than radioactivity!'

Holiness has often been identified solely with sexual repression. This is sometimes based on the assumption that only the world of the Spirit is good. The Greeks talked of the inherent evil of the body and the Victorians never talked of sex – both views are still around today. Sex is somehow not very holy and God just about tolerates it. Indeed, some Christians see sex purely for procreation in order to be 'fruitful and increase in number' (Gen 1:28).

Even the great theologian Augustine, early in the history of the Church, interpreted the struggle against evil as the struggle against sexuality and that sexual feelings were the result of the fall. He believed therefore that Adam was not turned on by Eve. He wrote, 'For my soul's freedom I resolved not to desire, nor to seek, nor to marry a wife.' What a contrast with the biblical view! 'God saw all that he had made and it was very good' (Gen 1:31) and that includes sex. The American writer Lewis Smedes sums this up when he says, 'to be wildly irrational, splendidly spontaneous and beautifully sensuous . . . is a gift'.

Of course an important component in God's plan for sex is the creation of new life, but notice that in this passage it is not procreation but intimacy that is central to God's purposes. The jazz artist Louis Armstrong once met the Pope. The Pope asked him, 'Do you have any children?' Armstrong replied, 'No, but we're having a lot of fun trying.'

Holy Christians need to affirm the goodness of sex. Discussion of sex is not unholy. The freeing of women's sexuality from the oppression of men is to be welcomed. God has given us sex for fun and intimacy. Unfortunately, in a world where men and women abuse God's gifts, many people have not experienced sex in this context. The child abused by someone they trusted, the woman brutally raped, the teenagers pressurised into sex by peer pressure or media, the mind warped by pornographic images showing women as mere sex objects, the couple unable to find fulfilment in the physical aspect of their relationship, are all often unable to see sex as good.

In such situations, God wants those who are victims to know his love and a new start. We must condemn all things which debase people and their sexuality. Through sympathy, counselling, therapy and relationships of trust, we must gently help each other to see that sex as God wants it is good and holy.

The exciting thing is that God does heal people and God does free people in this area. Not only through professional counselling but also through being part of the church where people experience unconditional love. I have the privilege as a pastor of seeing it all the time. Sophie was abused as a child and raped as an adult. She is a survivor who through her own courage and trust in God is defeating her fear, her bad self-image, her guilt and her negative view of sex. She still struggles and life is not easy, but God has given her new confidence and a sense of a new start to her life. From being at the point of suicide, she is now an outstanding Christian leader and her life speaks of the change that Jesus can bring.

2. Sex is given a context

Alongside the celebration of the goodness of sex, it is clear that God gives a certain context to this becoming of one flesh. In fact the goodness cannot be separated from the context.

Genesis 2:24 has the following elements of God's given context for sex:

- One flesh is God given. God gives the capacity for sexual relationship and indeed brings the man and woman together.
- One flesh is about one man and one woman.
- One flesh has a social context. The leaving of the father and mother is both a public act and a transfer of primary commitment.

- One flesh is about personal commitment. The man and the woman are to be united.

The traditional understanding of Christian marriage traces its origin back to this passage. Of course the Western institution of marriage understood in economic and social terms is a relatively recent creation. However, it attempts to embody these principles for one flesh given in creation.

The result of one flesh in this context is peace and intimacy, without shame or embarrassment (2:25). This is where the Bible starts with sex. It is very positive about sex in its God-given context, as a way of human intimacy, fun and companionship. Having said that, we need to be clear that due to our rebellion against God, God's ideal plan in creation becomes distorted. That which is meant to be good can often become the source of pain, guilt, embarrassment, disease and abuse. That which is good in its correct context becomes not good in another.

There are sexual relationships and uses of our sexuality which fall below God's ideal context of a committed, intimate, public and personal relationship of a man and a woman. On this basis, adultery, casual sex, premarital sex and homosexual sex are seen as sin in other parts of Scripture.

There is of course a degree of debate within the Christian community concerning certain questions about sex. There are those who maintain that the Bible's condemnation of homosexual sex is a condemnation of casual sex, rather than the committed relationship between two people of the same sex. However, the context of the deep relationship of one flesh seems to be clearly between a man and a woman.

Other debate centres on what should be the level of premarital sex for Christian couples. How far do you go? Do you stop before sexual intercourse, or where else do you draw the line – oral sex, mutual masturbation, kissing, or even holding hands? Some devise elaborate schemes for what is right or wrong, for example those who say no touching of the parts of the body that one would normally cover. On this view, the soles of the feet are a very dangerous place to touch! Others point out that even holding hands can be an intensely erotic experience, and stress the intention behind the specific action. As a young Christian I found myself reading every book on the subject, wanting a rule for every situation and then making what seemed to me to be every mistake. Even when Alison and I began the relationship that would lead to our marriage in our late and mid twenties, experience and a degree of maturity did not make the questions any easier. Even now I find it difficult when students and teenagers want me to give detailed advice on what is right and wrong.

I do worry about becoming too liberal in my old age of mid-thirties! But it does seem to me that we need to be careful in going beyond the Bible's teaching, forgetting the important principles by setting up an intricate system of rules. Such rules can protect people but they can also replace holiness with dead religion.

We need to respect God's given context for sex, understanding the importance of the level of personal commitment and the public aspect of that commitment. It seems clear that sexual intercourse should be left for marriage, and the Church through organisations like True Love Waits and honest teaching about sex can support young people in making decisions that the rest of society may not understand. At the same time physical contact is fun and builds a degree of intimacy. In my relationship with my wife before marriage we tried to ask each other the following questions:

- Is our physical relationship growing more than our emotional, intellectual and spiritual relationship?
- Are we comfortable under God with the level of our physical relationship?
- Are we both happy with where we are or is one person pushing the other too far?
- Are we praying about our relationship?

In all of this, Christian couples need to constantly talk with each other. It is often easier to find time to snog rather than talk and pray!

Masturbation is not dealt with in any detail in the Bible. Younger people often struggle with feelings of guilt that it is the 'greatest sin' built on language of 'self-abuse' to playground stories that it will make you go blind. The reality is that virtually all men masturbate at some times in their lives and a growing majority of women acknowledge that they do too.

We need to recognise masturbation for what it is. The sexual thrill and satisfaction is only a small part of what God intended. Masturbation is not meant to take over our lives as an addiction, stopping us from forming real relationships, and at the same time it does not need to cripple our Christian lives with guilt.

More serious is the link between masturbation and pornography. The vast bulk of pornographic images are made by men for men. Women are treated no longer as persons with their own inherent value and rights, but as sexual objects simply there to pleasure men. This cheapens sex, and the industry makes huge profits out of other people's bodies. The danger of masturbation and pornography is that men become 'blind' to seeing women as God-created and God-loved people. It breeds a view of women which in the extreme leads to rape and abuse.

Indeed, few things are worse than sexual abuse. The sexual abuse by those in power over others, whether the older man abusing the young child, the violent attack using physical strength to take sexual satisfaction from a woman, the emotional blackmail of another person into having sex, or the boss who sexually harasses employees – all are serious abuses of God's gift of sexuality. Such things happen in the Church as well as the world and must be stopped. A holy church is not where things are swept under the carpet but where men and women, boys and girls are protected, safe from harm.

This distorted context of sexual expression may be the result of our choices or may be imposed upon us. We need to remember that with God there is judgement, healing, forgiveness and consequences. There is forgiveness for those who commit adultery, although they may then have to live with the consequences of broken relationship. There is God's healing for those who have been abused.

In the past few years, along with many other churches, we have begun to take these things more seriously and talk about them openly. We have a clearly defined policy for all who work with children and young people. Those who have been convicted of offences against children cannot work with children. Some have criticised us on whether this represents a gospel of forgiveness and a new start. But the gospel of Jesus is also about protecting the vulnerable and we want to take every precaution to make sure that this protection is given.

As we have talked openly, I have found it amazing to see just how many people are able to share honestly that they are or have been victims. They speak about these experiences in carefully selected environments of professional counselling or close friendships. In this God is able to heal.

God also gives help in the struggle against temptation. God does this not only in our personal prayer but through being real with fellow Christians whom we trust. As a student, my friend Pete and I would share our temptations, our mistakes and our questions and then pray for one another. We would talk about the joy and pain of relationships. That was essential for me and I thank God for it.

3. Sex is not everything

In the Western world it is difficult to see beyond sex. Germaine Greer is quite right to emphasise that young women's lives should not be dominated by constant images of sex and getting the right boyfriend. Men too do not become fully human if they are totally dominated by sex.

The common misunderstanding of sex is that once you master the right technique then you will be happy. There is much more to becoming one flesh than intercourse. Intimacy in relationship is about communication, humour, discovery, growth, sharing, sacrifice, serving and working together.

In a society dominated by sex, it is easy to dismiss the value of friendship or family love in favour of sexual love. Those who choose to be single, or by circumstances are single are often classed as somehow odd by both the world and the church. In fact, one third of the people in the UK are single.

Our church here in Liverpool has constantly struggled over how to avoid alienating single people. Single people do a massive amount of work for the church but often feel a lack of support. We used to have monthly 'family services' until a single woman told me how difficult she found them – not the style of worship but the very name. They seemed to imply that you had to come with your family and she did not have any in Liverpool. We now call them 'all-age worship'. We make the mistake of seeing single people as 'not yet married' or 'post marriage' as if a sexual relationship was the high point of our humanity.

Yet the early chapters of Genesis show that men and women have much more to do than just becoming one flesh. As we shall see later in Chapter 12, human beings are given the responsibility of stewards of the earth in providing for one another, caring for the earth and exploring creation. Human beings are called into an intimate relationship with God, which although broken by disobedience can be restored in Jesus. In fact, the New Testament sees men and women reaching other men and women with this good news of new life with God through Jesus.

Sex is a part of what we are, it is not the only thing. It is easy to get hung up on sex, and forget the importance of friendships, our responsibilities to society as a whole, our human creativity in art or science and our relationship with God. To get sex in perspective helps enormously. Singleness is not a sub-holy state, nor is it more holy than those who are married. Sometimes people are single simply because of the circumstances of the world and their own lives. Sometimes people are single because of their own positive choice. Sometimes people are single as they respond to a specific calling from God. Jesus himself was fully human yet single.

At the same time, God's perspective on sex will remind us that sexual misconduct is not the unforgivable or most important sin. It is sin, but in a Victorian holiness we have often given the impression that masturbation is far more serious than hypocrisy or leaving sisters and brothers to starve. God's perspective of love and justice means that the Church must stand for sex in God's context, but at the same time repent for its own sin in the discrimination and lack of serving love towards homosexuals and teenagers who find themselves pregnant.

When my wife Alison was a teacher at a community college, she did a survey with a group of fourteen to sixteen year olds to find out where information about sex came from. Most of the teenagers admitted that it came from friends and teenage magazines, but the surprising result was that most said that they would prefer to have more information from parents. Therefore the college arranged an open evening for parents to see and talk through the sex education module used with these teenagers. However, less than 15 per cent of the parents bothered to turn up. The parents did not want the responsibility.

It is easy to stand on the sidelines and condemn. I feel at times like those parents, wanting someone else to get involved and help. It is easier to preach a sermon about the sin of pre-marital sex than to baby-sit the single person's child who needs to get out for the night.

Study and action

One book to read: N. Pollock, *The Relationships Revolution* (IVP: Leicester, 1998).

One outline for discussion:

1. How can your local fellowship give greater support to Christians in the area of sexuality?
2. How has the Church influenced your own understanding of sexuality?
3. How have the media influenced your own understanding of sexuality?
4. How can your local fellowship help those who are victims?

One question for yourself: What is the thing that God most wants to happen in this area of my life?

One action to take: Find a Christian who you can trust, share and pray with about mistakes and hopes for holiness in this area of your life. Meet occasionally to chat and pray.

7

HOLY YOURSELF

The telephone call from MTV came during the evening meal when we had a few students round. MTV wanted me to do an interview as part of a movie show. Such calls are not usual and my first thought was not about content or opportunity but what I should wear. I am not a natural MTV dresser, and my wife, children and the students were their usual helpful selves! I should buy myself a new shirt, or maybe a new suit and don't forget the shoes. I needed to be trendy but not too trendy as I wasn't 'exactly young'. The students offered to take me out shopping. My wife offered to take me out shopping. Even Hannah, my three-year-old daughter offered to take me out shopping, and she did not even understand what this was about!

I am not sure that I did either. Why is what we wear so important? Could the deep truths of the Christian gospel be better communicated by what I was wearing? There is a part of me that rebels against those type of questions. Yet as a pastor and an evangelist, I choose what I wear quite carefully to be true to who I am and to respect the context. But I am also conscious that I have to make these choices increasingly influenced by a fashion-obsessed society.

In the movie *Clueless,* Alicia Silverstone plays sixteen-year-old Cher who is a classic 'airhead'. Every morning she sits at her computer in her room and chooses her day's wardrobe. As David Bowie's *Fashion* plays in the background she matches belts, dresses and shoes with commands such as 'Browse' and 'Autodress' and a screen saver featuring a pattern of floating coat-hangers. This very clever parody of the obsession with fashion was a huge hit in the US. Publicity for the movie stated, 'Clothes offer Cher the energy, sense of continuity and spiritual fulfilment otherwise lacking in her life.'

Clueless plays on the increasing obsession in Western societies with fashion and the deeper question of image. Supermodels earn huge wages, and fashion features in many television programmes from the simple make-over to how to buy a whole new wardrobe. The A to Z of fashion from Alexander McQueen to zips fill magazines, whether for older women, new lads or young children. In one magazine a problem page had an earnest inquirer asking, 'Will my patent leather bag look outdated this winter?' And in case any men might have a self-satisfied smirk, a recent issue of *Esquire* had at least 20 per cent of its pages devoted to fashion or fashion advertising, including how to shine the perfect shoe, designer suits, weekend bags, technical outerwear, and modular furniture.

Why do we dress the way we do? There are many answers – to attract others, to influence others, to make ourselves popular, to conform to those around us or to rebel against them. One woman said, 'I dress for men, but I feel incredibly embarrassed about it.' The designer Jasper Conran said, 'This is who I am, this is where my head is.' For all of these reasons, advertisers can cleverly tap in and make us buy.

However, there are deeper reasons. We might believe that the image we portray is about 'making a statement' but many of us are controlled in what we wear by basic insecurity about ourselves. We hide behind the image. The journalist Sally Brampton wrote, 'Every woman in the world dresses, first and foremost, for the fat police.' Many would disagree with her, yet there is some truth about us hiding behind our image.

We long for the perfect appearance. A recent survey concluded that the 'perfect man' had George Clooney's hair, George Michael's teeth and Ewan McGregor's looks. The 'perfect woman' had amongst others things Calista Flockhart's hair and Imogen Stubbs' eyebrows. Most of us do not quite match these physical characteristics. So we try through many things from the gym to sunglasses to aspire to them. In fact for some, the question of image becomes very dangerous. I have spoken with a large number of younger women who are affected by depression, bulimia and anorexia. The stick-like images of supermodels are not the sole reason for their illnesses, but it does not help to have a society which seems to dictate image so much.

What does it mean to be holy in this area? Sackcloth and ashes or John the Baptist's new style for the season in camel's hair? At the other extreme are those Christian leaders who seem to witness to the plentiful provision of the Lord through designer suits and jewellery.

In fact, if we read on in Genesis after the passage of the previous chapter we see an interesting account of the first clothes and what it means to live in the knowledge of being made in the image of God:

Now the serpent was more crafty than any of the wild animals the Lord God had made. He said to the woman, 'Did God really say, "You must not eat from any tree in the garden"?'

[2]The woman said to the serpent, 'We may eat fruit from the trees in the garden, [3]but God did say, "You must not eat fruit from the tree that is in the middle of the garden, and you must not touch it, or you will die."'

[4]'You will not surely die,' the serpent said to the woman. [5]'For God knows that when you eat of it your eyes will be opened, and you will be like God, knowing good and evil.'

[6]When the woman saw that the fruit of the tree was good for food and pleasing to the eye, and also desirable for gaining wisdom, she took some and ate it. She also gave some to her husband, who was

with her, and he ate it. [7]Then the eyes of both of them were opened, and they realised that they were naked; so they sewed fig leaves together and made coverings for themselves.

[8]Then the man and his wife heard the sound of the Lord God as he was walking in the garden in the cool of the day, and they hid from the Lord God among the trees of the garden. [9]But the Lord God called to the man, 'Where are you?'

[10]He answered, 'I heard you in the garden, and I was afraid because I was naked; so I hid.'

[11]And he said, 'Who told you that you were naked? Have you eaten from the tree from which I commanded you not to eat?' [12]The man said, 'The woman you put here with me – she gave me some fruit from the tree, and I ate it.'

[13]Then the Lord God said to the woman, 'What is this you have done?' The woman said, 'The serpent deceived me, and I ate.'

(Genesis 3:1–13)

[20]Adam named his wife Eve, because she would become the mother of all the living.

[21]The Lord God made garments of skin for Adam and his wife and clothed them. [22]And the Lord God said, 'The man has now become like one of us, knowing good and evil. He must not be allowed to reach out his hand and take also from the tree of life and eat, and live for ever.' [23]So the Lord God banished him from the Garden of Eden to work the ground from which he had been taken. [24]After he drove the man out, he placed on the east side of the Garden of Eden cherubim and a flaming sword flashing back and forth to guard the way to the tree of life.

(Genesis 3:20–24)

Men and women reflect the image of God (Gen 1:26). That is not to say that we physically look like God, but we share with him responsibility, relationship and creativity. In Genesis 2, as we have seen in the previous chapter, there is beautiful peace and acceptance of one another, the 'man and the woman were both naked, and they felt no shame' (Gen 2:25).

It is interesting to speculate on whether if human beings had not fallen from God's plan, then would they still be naked? Indeed, should churches follow the naturists' line? Of course there is no answer, but the principle of being made in the image of God is that creativity is part of our humanity. There is a part of clothing which is about creativity – adding to beauty and expressing our personality. On this basis there is nothing unholy about expressing creativity in hair or fashion. Indeed it can be welcomed as enriching to our culture.

However, things begin to go wrong. Tempted by the serpent, Adam and Eve eat fruit from the only tree that God had instructed them not to eat, the tree of the knowledge of good and evil (Gen 3:1–6). The result is that their nakedness led to shame and they made coverings out of leaves (3:7). It is a pathetic picture of humanity affected by sin, rebelling against God. The Old Testament scholar Derek Kidner says, 'sin's proper fruit is shame'. It leads into what another scholar, David Atkinson, describes as a 'sense of unease at the heart of your being'. And if you are not comfortable with yourself then you will not be comfortable in the presence of someone else.

Sin means that people feel worthless and vulnerable within their very humanity. As God walks in the garden, Adam hides and replies, 'I was afraid because I was naked' (3:10). In this sense clothes do hide us in our shame from one another. We use our clothes not only to express our creativity and personality, but to do the very opposite – to hide our real selves from one another. Of course it is not just clothes. Due to our vulnerability, each of us projects an image which is based on fashion, the things we say, and how we manipulate other people.

However, the picture is a little more complicated than that. After the Lord pronounces the consequences of their sin, there is a lovely picture of God's continued care for men and women. 'The Lord God made garments of skin for Adam and his wife and clothed them' (3:21). It is a picture of God's generosity to us even in our sin.

From the perspective of the New Testament it is a reminder

of what God has done for us in Christ. As we saw in Chapter 4, Paul uses the imagery of clothing to encourage us to 'put off' the old self and 'put on' the new self, the clothing of righteousness, acceptance, forgiveness, love, peace, and power achieved by the death of Jesus on the cross. The consequence of this is that we are loved so much that Jesus died for us and we are now accepted by God through faith in him. No longer alienated and afraid of God, we stand in the right clothes to be in his holy presence.

In our shame and sin God gives us new clothes to wear. These 'spiritual' clothes can give us new confidence in life. Part of my debate about what to wear at MTV was in order that I felt relaxed and confident and able to use the opportunity to the full. But at a deeper level, as I have learnt of the new clothes that God has given me it has allowed me to be relaxed in his presence and in the presence of others.

Naomi had a great deal of problems with her own self-image. She seemed outwardly confident and mature as a Christian but inwardly was fearful of how others viewed her and how God viewed her. She had an eating disorder which she carefully hid from others through a number of methods such as arriving late at mealtimes and not eating with others. If she did eat she would make herself sick later. She cut herself on her arms and legs with knives as an attempt to cry out for help. Practically she had to wear long baggy clothes that hid these scars and her thin body. She doubted whether God could love her and reacted to preaching that said God's love was universal by saying, 'True for everyone else but not me – I'm the exception.'

As with many stories of people that God has touched that I have told in this book, her healing was not a sudden experience. There were special moments along the way when the Spirit of God touched her life whether in floods of tears or leaps of joy. But as she learned more of God's love shown in his death on the cross and saw that same love in Christians around her, she developed the courage to move on. It has been a slow process which still continues. She has learnt strategies to deal with her eating disorder and God is healing her self-image. As this has happened her great gifts have developed more depth. Many people now go to her for advice, support and prayer. She has learnt new confidence with her new clothes from God.

Let me try to apply this biblical understanding to some practical questions. How do we keep our balance and be holy in the area of fashion and image?

1. Be yourself

It is quite difficult to be yourself in a world obsessed with image. Liza Minelli once said, 'I've always felt like I didn't exist unless I was defined through a man's eyes,' and Raquel Welch said, 'I am just a piece of meat . . . I fulfil the ambitions of other people to make money out of me.' The great comic actor Peter Sellers claimed before his death, 'I haven't a clue who Peter Sellers is.'

In contrast, knowing the one who created you, who loves you and has died for you, sets you free to be yourself. A young black American, rebelling against inferiority feelings put on him by whites, proclaimed, 'I'm me and I'm good, 'cause God don't make junk.'

An older man was dying of cancer and the church music group went into his hospital room to sing songs of worship with him. In one of the songs they changed the words and sang as if God himself was saying this to the man:

> 'My child, you are more precious than silver,
> My child, you are more costly than gold,
> My child you are more beautiful than diamonds,
>   and nothing I desire compares to you.'

For those who trust in Christ there is no need to hide, or to conform because of insecurity. There is no need to make a statement in the hope of being loved. We are created in the image of

God, redeemed by God and loved absolutely by God. Part of that creation is creativity with clothes and we are all called to enrich the beauty of this world with this creativity.

At the age of two years old our daughter Hannah began to decide what she was going to wear each day. Even at that young age she wanted to express herself through what she wore. She did come up with some interesting combinations but we were pleased that she wanted to express herself – sometimes!

Indeed, God loves diversity. I love looking at our congregation while they are worshipping. Some are in their 'Sunday best' of suits and dresses. Others are in football shirts and jeans. Some occasionally wear characteristic clothes of their country of origin. Some wear designer labels and some do not. Some preach in dog collars and some preach in baseball caps. I rejoice in the diversity!

I fear the times when we try to make people conform to one image of what it means to be a Christian, rather than allowing diversity and creativity. Holiness means rejoicing in what God has given us.

2. Keep a sense of perspective

We should not get hung up on sex and we should not get hung up on clothes. There is more to life than being coat-hangers for clothes! Jesus expressed it as: 'Is not life more important than food, and the body more important than clothes?' (Mt 6:25). So Jesus continues, why worry about clothes, as God will clothe you. But seek first his kingdom. This poses us with the question of how much time and money do we spend on clothes and image?

The magazines and television ads insist on make-up, hair styles, fashion and even cosmetic surgery because we 'are worth it'. Yet we need to see these things in their proper perspective. Cosmetic surgery can help some with poor self-image, but as the way to eternal youth can quickly become an idol.

In the West in the past few decades there has been a tremendous growth in the popularity of health and fitness. Gyms are opening everywhere. I go to a gym two or three times a week. I realised a few years ago that I was not looking after my body as a gift from God and I find I am constantly battling against being overweight. Yet the desire for a beautiful body can go beyond mere stewardship of what God has given to become an obsession. If we see our self-worth only in terms of an attractive body clothed with designer garments then it is very poor.

Holiness encourages us to see the bigger picture of our self-worth and creativity in the context of the building of God's kingdom.

3. Dress appropriately

Of course there will be social constraints and expectations which Christian love will demand us to respect. The demands of a job, respect for a public occasion and the danger of distracting and tempting others will need to be treated with common sense.

Paul instructs Timothy on what this means in the local church, 'I want women to dress modestly, with decency and propriety, not with braided hair or gold or pearls or expensive clothes, but with good deeds appropriate for women who profess to worship God' (1Tim 2:9). Today I am sure that he would warn men to be just as careful in their dress.

The greatest beauty that men and women have is in Jesus shining out through you. Paul is worried about undue distraction of others in worship. I know that I should not be distracted in worship by such things. After all I am a minister! But the reality is that I do struggle. At a communion service recently while I was giving bread to a group of people who were kneeling in front of me, one woman's low-cut dress meant that I wasn't thinking about the body of Christ but whether I would fumble and drop the bread down the front of her dress!

On a more positive note the way we dress can express our respect for the occasion. The folk in our church who wear their best suits for worship are saying that worship is the most important thing of the week.

Holiness is not just about ourselves, it is a corporate thing. We need to ask whether the way we dress will influence others for good or bad.

4. Don't judge people by what they wear

If younger people need to heed words about appropriate dress, then perhaps older people especially need to heed the biblical teaching of not discriminating on account of clothing. In the letter of James, the author talks about how attitudes in a church can depend on how a person is dressed. He points out that how people are dressed, or how rich they might or might not be does not reflect the inner quality of faith (Jas 2:2–5).

A visiting preacher once told off one of our leaders for wearing jeans to church on a Sunday. He felt that the young man was not showing enough respect for the occasion. In fact the leader had just finished an all-night shift and it was quite a sacrifice to be at church at all that morning. The preacher had made the mistake of judging a person's commitment by the clothes they were wearing. In fact, the preacher wearing a cassock, a gown and a scarf on a warm sunny day might be interpreted as stupidity rather than respect for worship! Clerical dress is no more holy than jeans, and after the service as they talked they understood more of each other. It is very easy to make judgements of other people on how they dress, particularly if they dress differently to us. Holiness looks beyond a standard or style of clothing.

On one occasion when I was speaking at the Greenbelt arts festival (a Christian open-air event held every summer in Britain) we all went as a family. I had had my usual difficulty in choosing what to wear. This was an arts festival for younger

people and I did not fit in! We arrived for the final day to find
the site swamped in mud. I found my new shoes and trousers
quickly covered in mud but worse was to follow. My wife had
taken our children to buy some Wellington boots in the local
town but the only ones that would fit my five-year-old son
Adam were bright pink with pictures of Barbie on the sides! He
was very happy with them but Dad was not – in my view they
were not for boys and anyway Barbie in such a festival would
surely be politically incorrect. We must have looked a right sight
sliding through the mud. My 'sensible' speaker clothes covered
from the knee down in mud, holding hands with a five-year-old
boy wearing Barbie boots. Yet we were accepted and welcomed
for who we were and what we could give. People looked beyond
the clothes to us as people.

5. Be ready to give to the needy

The fashion frenzy of the West is a huge industry. We spend
massive amounts of money on clothing for all different reasons.
There should be times, however, when we remember those in
need. In the parable of the sheep and the goats, Jesus speaks of
the poor in terms of needing clothes (Mt 25:31–46). It is a
judgement on those who are comfortable and self-centred and
do not see that holiness means practical action for those in
need.

Do you have opportunities to share what God has given you?
Some share baby clothes with other families with young children, some churches provide cheap clothes for the community
through sales. We can support the work of charity shops
through giving clothes and clearing out our unused wardrobes.
We do not need to express our creativity and self-expression
only in designer labels made by the exploitation of workers in
sweat shops. We can express it through buying clothes, jewellery
and make-up through fair trade companies such as Traidcraft.

As a student in Cambridge I remember buying a coat in an

Oxfam shop for a good price. I was so pleased with it for it was very 'Cambridge student' rather than my old coat which my wife later christened a 'walking duvet'. The first night I wore the new coat I was walking through central Cambridge when I saw a man sitting in the cold beside a college entrance. He simply said, 'It's cold, can I have your coat?' Embarrassed and wanting to keep my coat, I walked on by literally on the other side. The next morning I rose to read my Bible and pray. The verse for the day was 'And if someone wants to sue you and take your tunic, let him have your coat as well . . . Give to the one who asks you, and do not turn away from the one who wants to borrow from you' (Mt 5:40–42). I knew to my shame that I had got my priorities wrong.

Study and action

One book to read: M. Starkey, *Fashion and Style* (Monarch: Crowborough, 1995).

One outline for discussion:
1. Where do you buy your clothes and why – does being a Christian make any difference?
2. Look at John 8:2–11. In this story what does Jesus do for this woman's self-image and the attitude of those around her?
3. Why do we so readily judge people by what they wear?
4. How can your local fellowship improve its expression of creativity, diversity and giving to the needy in the area of clothes and fashion?

One question for yourself: How secure are you in knowing that you are loved by God?

One action to take: Look at the clothes in your wardrobe in the light of this chapter – decide which to keep, which to throw away and which to give away.

8

IS IT HOLIER TO BE RICH OR POOR?

Money is a very powerful thing. When Abba sang, 'Money, money, money . . . it's a rich man's world', they were simply expressing a fact experienced by rich and poor alike.

This Abba song from some years ago may not be great poetry, but it is very perceptive. The world is an economic world. The song itself was part of a series of songs which earned the Swedish pop group millions. It reflects the late 1970s and 1980s and its obsession with wealth. Ronald Reagan and Margaret Thatcher headed governments which believed in the free market, allowing unemployment to rise so that taxes and inflation could stay low. The fall of communism gave rise to new capitalist economies in Eastern Europe. Madonna sang that we were 'living in a material world, and I am a material girl'. Of course it has always been the case to varying degrees that 'money makes the world go around', but perhaps never more so than in the last three decades.

The nineties by contrast may have been much more of a caring decade, but money is supreme. In many countries the rich have become richer and the poor poorer. The introduction of a National Lottery and scratchcards into the UK highlighted our insatiable greed for wealth. The big finger pointing from the sky and saying, 'It could be you' is believed to be the way to happiness, peace and security.

It seems that such an obsession with money has had a profound effect on how some Christians look at money. This is demonstrated by two extreme approaches.

a) Health and wealth?

The first is what is often called the prosperity gospel. To oversimplify it, this is the teaching which says that if you lead a holy life then God will bless you with health, wealth and happiness. Every Christian has the possibility of becoming a millionaire if they have enough faith. This is built on the claim that the Bible is positive about prosperity. Certain books will quote Joshua 1:7–8, 'Be careful to obey all the law my servant Moses gave you; do not turn from it to the right or to the left, that you may be successful . . . then you will be prosperous and successful', to support such a claim.

This teaching is especially popular in the USA and South Korea, and often tends to be connected with charismatic churches. While in South Korea I remember talking to a young Christian from one of the largest churches in the world. We were talking about how God blesses us and I expressed scepticism that he wanted to give us financial wealth. She immediately got out her Bible, looked up 2 Corinthians 8:9 and read 'For your sakes he became poor, so that you through his poverty might become rich,' and said, 'There you are, what do you make of that?'

The argument goes that because God has promised wealth and success for his people, we can receive it either by claiming his promises or living holy lives. If we are poor then the fault lies with us either because of doubt or because of sin. Various books appear in the Christian market telling stories of remarkable faith which leads to material wealth, or the way a small offering to the Lord is repaid in terms of income hundreds and thousands times that of the original gift. That is quite extreme, but the view is also expressed in a more subtle way. We assume that God should bless us in a material way, so we look down at other Christians who get into debt, whose businesses go bankrupt or those who are unemployed.

b) Simplicity and poverty

At the other extreme is the 'simple living' gospel. In simple terms this is to say that you cannot be holy and rich. No Christian should be a millionaire, indeed poverty is the way for the Christian. It seems on first glance just as biblical as the prosperity gospel. Jesus said, 'Blessed are you who are poor, for yours is the kingdom of God' (Lk 6:20) and, 'Sell your possessions and give to the poor' (Lk 12:33). Once again examples are put forward of holy people who have given up all their wealth, such as Francis of Assisi. This teaching too has its extremes, illustrated by one Puritan's attitude to the celebration of Christmas. In the seventeenth century Hezekiah Woodward called it, 'the old heathens' feasting day, in honour to Saturn their God, the papist's massing day, the profane man's ranting day, the superstitious man's idol day, the multitude's idle day . . . the true Christian man's fasting day'.

It is on the basis of this teaching that I feel extremely guilty about spending any money at all on myself. My family despair of my inability to think that money spent on clothes or leisure is a 'good use' of it. I have this inner feeling that money should only be spent for others and in some ways is basically unholy.

I have been a minister to churches where the people have been very affluent and churches where they have not been too well off. I began preaching with the naivety of having been a student most of my life, and saw money as a bad thing. On one occasion I was taken aside by a man in the church whose car and clothes spoke of some considerable wealth. He said that he had difficulty with the impression I had given that the holy way to live was to give all your wealth away. He could do that but it would also lead to the 'giving away' of forty jobs in his company and the lives of the families who would be affected by that. Immediately afterwards another person took me aside and said that they had nothing to give away and indeed their lack of money was not a 'holy state' but a state which denied them basic opportunities within our society.

It was beginning to get a little more complicated. It became even more horrendously complicated when I got married and we had children! The responsibility to others, the need to use resources well and plan ahead have driven me back to re-examine the simplistic views that I had had as a student. What is a biblical attitude to money? What does it mean to be holy earners, savers and spenders? In the following three passages Paul speaks about these questions to his young colleague Timothy and in them I find a lovely balance to help me walk through the complexity.

The Spirit clearly says that in later times some will abandon the faith and follow deceiving spirits and things taught by demons. [2]Such teachings come through hypocritical liars, whose consciences have been seared as with a hot iron. [3]They forbid people to marry and order them to abstain from certain foods, which God created to be received with thanksgiving by those who believe and who know the truth. [4]For everything God created is good, and nothing is to be rejected if it is received with thanksgiving, [5]because it is consecrated by the word of God and prayer.

(1 Timothy 4:1–5)

[6]But godliness with contentment is great gain. [7]For we brought nothing into the world, and we can take nothing out of it. [8]But if we have food and clothing, we will be content with that. [9]Those who want to get rich fall into temptation and a trap and into many foolish and harmful desires that plunge people into ruin and destruction. [10]For the love of money is a root of all kinds of evil.

Some people, eager for money, have wandered from the faith and pierced themselves with many griefs.

(1 Timothy 6:6–10)

[17]Command those who are rich in this present world not to be arrogant nor to put their hope in wealth, which is so uncertain, but to put their hope in God, who richly provides us with everything for our enjoyment. [18]Command them to do good, to be rich in good deeds, and to be generous and willing to share. [19]In this way they will lay up treasure for themselves as a firm foundation for the coming age, so that they may take hold of the life that is truly life.

(1 Timothy 6:17–19)

1. The importance of thanksgiving

In the first passage Paul was writing to Timothy about a very serious attack on the Christian faith. It was the belief that everything in the material world was bad. Only the spiritual was good. So sex, money, parties, leisure and material possessions were things of the flesh rather than the spirit. They led you away from God and should not be part of the holy life. Such attitudes, as we have already seen, are still around today in Christian circles. Paul says that these false teachers 'forbid people to marry and order them to abstain from certain foods' (v3). His reply is 'rubbish!' In fact he is much stronger than that, saying such teachings come from demons and liars (vv1–2). It is a perversion of the fact that God has created this material world. 'For everything God created is good, and nothing is to be rejected if it is received with thanksgiving' (v4).

The material world is there to be used wisely, but it is there to be enjoyed. Jesus himself demonstrates this in the Gospels. It seems he loved parties such as weddings (John 2:1–11), and he dined with the prosperous as well as the poor. After all, a tax collector like Zacchaeus would not receive many guests (Lk 19:1–10). Perhaps because of this, his enemies accused him of being a glutton and a drunkard (Mt 11:19). Even on the night when he was betrayed, his institution of a symbol by which his disciples would remember him was at a meal with bread and wine.

God wants his people to celebrate the glorious goodness of his creation. The key to getting our attitude right is thanksgiving. Constant thanksgiving reminds us that all that we have comes from the Lord. This helps us to use it wisely. We cannot deny that we live in a world dominated by economics, but we can earth it by constant thanksgiving. One woman having grasped this truth returned to her home and went round her house sayings things like, 'Lord, thank you for this television, it is yours not mine', 'Lord, thank you for this cheque book and the money it represents, Lord, it is yours not mine', 'Lord, thank you for this bed, it is yours not mine.'

2. The danger of idolatry

We now pick up Paul's later argument in 1 Timothy 6:6–10. The reaction to the false teaching that the material world is bad, can go to the opposite extreme. That is to see no danger in it at all, and Paul is rightly worried about this position.

Creation is good, but human beings are dominated by the principle of sin which sees us abuse creation. We constantly confuse need with greed. Paul contrasts the contentment of having sufficient in terms of food and clothing (vv7–8) with the desires and cravings of wanting more, more, more.

The philosopher Schopenhauer once observed, 'Gold is like sea water – the more one drinks of it, the thirstier one becomes.' The pursuit of riches can cause a person to fall into temptation and an ultimate trap of ruin and destruction. The actress Liz Hurley commented, 'Everyone I know who has inherited money is totally round the bend.' Christians say that everyone whose sole pursuit in life is money is in danger. Why? Because money takes over from God as the centre of our lives. It becomes an idol or a god-substitute. We believe that it will give us value, happiness and future security, but we are wrong.

In the early years of our marriage we lived on one income and survived. As our income has increased in recent years it has been difficult to stop the extravagance of our lifestyle growing too. I am constantly reminded of the Methodist preacher John Wesley who over many years while his income increased kept his expenditure exactly the same.

When Jesus was approached by a man who has come to be known as the 'rich young ruler' (Lk 18:18–30), the man asked him the way to eternal life. Having kept the commandments, Jesus asked him to sell all his possessions and give the money to the poor. Luke comments, 'When he heard this, he became very sad, because he was a man of great wealth. Jesus looked at him and said, "How hard it is for the rich to enter the kingdom of God! Indeed, it is easier for a camel to go through the eye of a needle than for the rich to enter the kingdom of God".'

Some commentators suggest that Jesus is referring here to a small gate in the walls of Jerusalem known as the eye of the needle, and how difficult it was to get camels through. That may be reading too much into it. Jesus may simply be using an extravagant humorous picture of a camel and a needle. What is clear is that he is talking of the dangers of riches.

The disciples are worried. They ask about who can be saved because they recognise that all are rich in some way. Jesus replies with an assurance that salvation is the work of God, not human beings. Seen in the light of the rich young ruler, Jesus is warning about money or possessions becoming an idol. Money will not save you, only God can. Eventually some realise this. The multimillionaire William Hearst was so insecure that he would not allow anyone to say the word death in his presence.

The rich young ruler was challenged by Jesus at the very point where he misunderstood what it meant to be right with God. For him his riches were his god, the centre of his life, dominating his thoughts and actions. Unable to give that up he went away very sad.

Paul is here echoing those words of Jesus concerning the danger of idolatry. In fact, he goes further, saying that such idolatry is not only dangerous, but also stupid. To paraphrase verse 7, you did not bring a bank balance or a Mercedes car into the world with you and will not take one out.

We once got a last-minute holiday bargain and went to Luxor on the Nile in Egypt. There stands the Valley of the Kings. We were taken round the vast tombs built for the kings of Egypt, consisting of numerous storage chambers intended to hold provisions and treasures for the next world. Yet the bodies eventually decayed, and the tombs were robbed. It was a graphic reminder that you cannot take it with you.

Is money my idol? I heard a preacher once say that a good test is to think about what your mind wanders to when you are daydreaming. For that is often your treasure. 'For where your treasure is, there your heart will be also' (Mt 6:21). It was one of those moments when the Holy Spirit seemed to single me out. I knew I would daydream about having enough money to be really comfortable. God had always given me what I needed when I needed it, but now I was putting my trust in lots of money rather than him. It was a painful lesson and I still continue to learn it.

To dethrone the idol means that Jesus has to be Lord. This will mean constant thanksgiving, confession for the times we let money take over, and the asking of God's guidance to be wise stewards of what he has given us. Perhaps most of all it involves generosity, something that we turn to next.

3. The needs of others

Paul now addresses 'those who are rich in this present world' (1 Tim 6:17). Some of us might feel tempted to skip this section! We may feel we are not rich at all, and perhaps we have some justification. We might be attempting the increasingly difficult job of making ends meet as a student. We may be struggling to keep up with mortgage payments. We might find ourselves crippled by debt. But we must always see ourselves in God's perspective.

As a research student I worked for a time in Bombay. I thought of myself as quite poor until I saw some of the real poverty in India. I remember arguing one night with a taxi driver who was attempting to overcharge me, probably because I was a foreigner. I suddenly realised I was arguing over such a small amount, indeed so small that back in the UK it would not even buy a small bar of chocolate. Yet for the taxi driver it was of a totally different value. As a 'poor' research student my lifestyle did not in the slightest way compare with real poverty. As we begin to see ourselves in the West in the context of God's world we begin to see that many more of us are rich in this world. For every 100 babies born in the world, 40 die before the age of six, 40 face the threat of damage because of malnutrition, and only three will be given skills and training.

Of course, poverty exists not only in India. Here in Liverpool many people are without jobs, homes, food, decent clothing, heat and light – things that many of us take for granted. Many times we have people come to church asking for small sums of money. We know that some want it for drugs or alcohol but others want it for electricity cards or gas for heating.

While researching a recent book on the millennium I was struck again at the vast number of biblical passages which are directly about God's concern for the poor.[1] The fact that God is so concerned is then reflected in how the rich are to live. Paul instructs Timothy, 'Command them to do good, to be rich in good deeds, and to be generous and willing to share' (v18). This is based on the command not to set their hopes on the uncertainty of riches but on God who provides for our enjoyment – a sense of thanksgiving and the danger of idolatry (v17).

Martin Luther once cheekily said, 'Money is like manure

. . . no good unless you spread it.' This is a command for all Christians, not just the millionaires. Bono, the lead singer of U2, once commented, 'If you are not committed to the poor, what is religion? It's a black hole.' Of course that does not mean that we have to give everything away. The needs of the poor can be met by wealth creation by those who run businesses providing jobs, services and a growing economy. Wealth creation needs to go hand in hand with just distribution. Do I have holy pockets? Does money go through and disappear, or is it used wisely and shared with those in need? An old preacher said the last part of man to be converted is his wallet. If he was preaching today he would no doubt have said that the last thing to be converted is a person's bank balance or credit card. I have to say that is often my experience. Other parts of the holy tightrope seem easier than this one.

We are all asked to 'live simply so that others can simply live'. That means good and wise planning of the use of our resources, consistent and committed giving to others, and a constant sense of the Lordship of Christ over our wealth. Some will be asked to go further in serving overseas or in serving alongside the poor.

Finally, love of money devalues us. The poet Ben Okri once said, 'We have been destroying ourselves through smallness. We have come to worship and enshrine the wrong things, the objects which we have produced. We prize our clothes above our thoughts, our appearances above our consciousness. We take more pride in our polish, our surface, than in learning two lines of a sonnet . . . We have made gods of lesser things, and, in doing so, it follows that we have made ourselves lower than these objects.'[2] As we make money our god, we lose God's perspective and wander away from the path of holiness.

Study and action

One book to read: R. Sider, *Rich Christians in an Age of Hunger* (Hodder: London, 1997).

One outline for discussion:

1. How can your local fellowship help Christians be better stewards of money?
2. How much of its income does your local fellowship give away compared to the amount it uses to improve its buildings or church life?
3. How can we stop money becoming an idol?
4. Who are the poor in your community?

One question for yourself: Is money your God?

One action to take: Work out the percentage of your income that you give away to others. If in the light of that, you feel you need to increase the percentage, make plans through covenants and regular giving commitments to do so.

Notes

1. R. Frost and D. Wilkinson, *A New Start? Hopes and Dreams for the New Millennium* (Hodder Headline: London, 1999).
2. *The Times Magazine* (2 January 1999), p. 12.

9

CAN YOU BE A HOLY ACCOUNTANT?

My son Adam wants to be a preacher, a professional footballer, an astronaut and singer in a band. At the age of five that might change! Recently we had work done on the house and Adam announced he wanted to be a workman. When we asked why, he replied that it would be good to spend all of your day having a drink and eating lots of biscuits!

Most of us dream about the ideal job consisting of short hours, no commuting, real responsibility and lots of money. A job where we are totally free to express our creativity and at the same time a job which will earn us respect from others. A recent survey by the dating agency Drawing Down the Moon asked potential partners about the most attractive jobs to the opposite sex. Men were attracted by women who worked in public relations, and women were attracted by male architects. The trouble is that very few of us work in such 'attractive jobs'. Many people work in dead-end jobs, full of tedium, poorly paid and in bad working conditions. Work is not an expression of our creativity, it is simply a chore. Oscar Wilde commented, 'Work is the curse of the drinking classes.' Many people see work as a necessary but unfortunate evil. It is seen as a means to an end, such as money, holidays and retirement. The pressures of time and urgent work, the insecurity of employment, and the fear of unemployment add to the stress of modern-day living.

Pubs and clubs are filled at the weekends with people trying to escape from the drudgery of work through alcohol, drugs, sex and excitement. Churches can be the same – giving people a 'fix' of faith in the evenings or on a Sunday. Often among Christians, work in the secular world is not given the same importance and status as 'full-time Christian' work such as the ordained ministry or evangelism. A friend of mine, explaining that he felt God had called him to his job, was greeted with the reply, 'Can you be a holy accountant?'

Some Christians see their work only as a means of support for the more important activities of church life or reaching others. Other Christians simply do not see the connection between what is done on a Sunday morning and what they do during the week. In that they are not helped by sermons and worship totally out of touch with real issues.

At the other extreme are those people for whom work is everything. If we find ourselves in this position, then we see work as the driving force in our lives giving us identity and purpose. Chris was a student at our church who grew in faith and had great gifts. He moved to London where he joined a big firm with some challenging work. He found great fulfilment in work and as he was good more opportunities came and work increased. He became important in the firm and respected by others because of his job. Other things such as church, friends and leisure were pushed out. Trying to find a new church was too time consuming. He no longer goes to church and his faith has not grown.

How do we walk the tightrope between these extremes and be holy in our work? The following passage in Colossians concerns an extreme case of work: slavery. As one commentator noted, if you can be holy in this, then you can be holy in anything!

[22]Slaves, obey your earthly masters in everything; and do it, not only when their eye is on you and to win their favour, but with sincerity of heart and reverence for the Lord. [23]Whatever you do, work at it with all your heart, as working for the Lord, not for human masters, [24]since you know that you will receive an inheritance from the Lord as a reward. It is the Lord Christ you are serving. [25]Those who do wrong will be repaid for their wrongs, and there is no favouritism.

4 Masters, provide your slaves with what is right and fair, because you know that you also have a Master in heaven.

(Colossians 3:22–4:1)

1. Holiness is worked out within fallen structures

Paul's advice is odd to modern readers. 'Slaves, obey your earthly masters in everything' (v22). The immediate question here is obvious. Why doesn't Paul object to slavery? Surely he should be saying, 'slaves run away, and masters repent!'

I have struggled with this, not only with Paul's apparent acceptance of slavery but also with what seems to be his self-contradiction. Famously he writes to the Galatians, 'There is neither Jew nor Greek, there is neither slave or free . . . for you are all one in Christ Jesus' (Gal 3:28). Indeed, freedom is a major theme of this letter (Col 2) and Paul echoes the Galatians passage (Col 3:11). He argues that in Christ you are free from the old inequalities, but how in practice does this work out?

It seems to me that different commentators point out many things in order to get Paul off the hook! Slavery in the ancient world did seem to be different to our current understanding of slavery based on the forced abduction, exile and structural exploitation of Africans. For example, slaves were freed after seven years, a slave hurt in any way became free, and for some slavery was a chosen profession. Others point out that it was such an accepted part of the world and essential to the whole economic and social structure, that for Paul to criticise it would be like criticising the motor car today. Yet there is enough elsewhere in the Bible and in Paul's writing to condemn slavery and of course Christians like William Wilberforce led the movement to condemn it.

However, it does seem here that Paul is making slavery worse. Slaves are not only to remain as slaves, they are to obey their masters in everything. We need to be very honest here, and acknowledge that Paul's purpose is not to condemn the institution of slavery. He has a different question in mind: what should be the attitude of a Christian who finds himself or herself within an institution? It is a passage not addressed to politicians but addressed to members of the Church.

Whether we are slaves or not, we are part of an imperfect world with imperfect structures. Some jobs that Christians find themselves in will be tedious and badly paid. Some will have expectations that are unrealistic. They will not always have Christian bosses or colleagues. Some will be treated unfairly.

What do we do? Do we say that we will have nothing to do with such jobs? I found myself on a convention platform recently in front of 3,000 people while the preacher denounced certain kinds of jobs which dehumanise people. He was arguing that jobs where human beings are simply used as factory machines should not be part of society. I agreed with him, but then found myself wondering what those in the audience who did have such jobs would be thinking. No doubt they would welcome the vision of the future, but on Monday morning when the convention finished they would be back in those jobs. Financial pressures would mean that they could not give the jobs up, so how can they work in those jobs in a holy way? That is the question Paul is addressing.

A Christian friend moved out of a secular job because the pressure and the need to compromise were too much. He thought by working full time for the Church his Christian life would improve and he would find fulfilment. After a year he found that stress and pain were also part of employment in the Church. Even the Methodist Church is a fallen structure!

Work is rooted in creation, in that God gives us the capacity to work (Gen 1:28), but it is also done in a fallen world. Full-time Christian work is to be done both in and outside the Church. It encompasses the preacher and the physicist, the environmentalist and the evangelist, the tax inspector and the theologian. The Reformers emphasised this clearly. They encouraged every Christian to see that they had a calling and that every legitimate vocation was pleasing to God. William Tyndale wrote, 'There is difference betwixt washing of dishes and preaching the word of God; but as touching to please God, none at all.' Many years later Dorothy L. Sayers echoed this by saying, 'The only Christian work is a good work well done.'

In Paul's statement of obedience to earthly masters he is encouraging us to work with all our hearts and minds. For whatever job we find ourselves in we are to do whatever is required of us to the best of our ability.

During my time as a scientist in the academic world, I once felt I had been given a raw deal by those over me. I felt so angry at the situation that I thought seriously about leaving. It seemed to me to be unfair and that I was being used. At that stage I would read my Bible and pray at lunchtime. Ready to write a letter of resignation, I thought I had better pray about it first. The passage for the day just happened to be Colossians 3:22–25, the one above. God seemed to be saying, this is where I want you to continue to work, and with all the frustrations to try and live a holy life.

We work as part of structures that many of us have no control over. The child is under a teacher, a student under a lecturer, the train driver under a supervisor, and the junior doctor under the consultant and hospital administrator. It can quite often feel like we are slaves to the structure or those above us. In those situations, what is God saying to us about holy work?

2. Holiness gives a distinctive motive

The power of superiors can be a dominant aspect of our work. We may have many motives for work such as promotion, to impress others, to do the minimun of effort in order to keep a job, to avoid a rebuke, or to keep in the boss's good books. As research students we knew that every morning our supervisor would wander round the offices at 9am to see if we were at our desks. If you were not there then he would leave you a memo noting your absence and giving you some extra work. So at 9am we were all at our desks – and after we had seen him we went over to the library for a leisurely morning coffee!

Paul's attitude is quite different. In verse 22 he encourages slaves to work not just when the eyes of superiors are on them. The Christian motive for work is primarily to work for the Lord (vv 23–24). We are to work with sincerity of heart, and with reverence for the Lord. Ultimately it is not yourself nor the company that you are serving, it is the Lord.

To work as Christians is to work for the Lord. Business is not done primarily for our bosses. Teaching is not done for inspectors, study is not solely to pass exams, even gardening is not merely done to placate your spouse! Now this is not to downplay the importance of accountability in jobs. Three students at my university became well known for not revising for their exams, because they wanted to 'trust the Lord, and witness to their lecturers'. However, the Lord trusted them to get on with their revision! They failed their exams and instead of a powerful witness, they gave evangelical Christians a bad name in the university for years to come.

Nevertheless, to see work as done primarily for the Lord gives a sense of freedom. If we work to the Lord, we work with enthusiasm but we are careful not to overwork. Christ is concerned for our whole person, and does not want us to squeeze out other important parts of our life. At the same time we should be concerned about daily faithfulness in our work, rather than simply catching the eye of our boss. Working for the Lord encourages responsibility in freedom.

In Paul's time, slaves who had been dehumanised by being called the property of other human beings, still saw themselves as servants and friends of the Lord. Today we experience, but are not bound, by the pressures of a job. When difficult ethical decisions come up, we need to have a sense of what is the right decision not for us, or the company but for the Lord. Our work can become not a source of frustration, or a desperate struggle for more money, but an act of worship.

Of course, to work for the Lord will at times be costly. We may get lower qualifications than those who cheat. We may be passed over for promotion because we are not prepared to let our work become our all-consuming idol. That is the cost of holy work. But God does promise that all work for him will be rewarded, in ways that lie beyond our imagination.

In my first degree which was physics, I worked very badly. I was very busy in Christian groups, I played a lot of sport and was very lazy towards my work. I remember often coming in from church on a Sunday night with work to be handed in for the next morning. I would sometimes copy from other people because I did not have the time to do the work myself. In studying for exams my motive was often to look good in my parents' eyes. I was fortunate to get a very high degree.

Some years later when I did a degree in theology I had learnt some of the lessons and tried not to make the same mistakes. I tried to do my work faithfully, not trying to impress anyone. I put far more work into it but came out with a lower result than in my first degree. Yet I have more satisfaction in the theology degree – it may have been a lower result but perhaps it was a holier result!

3. Holiness leads to responsibility

Paul does not underestimate the difficulties of this kind of teaching. Indeed, in giving this teaching he was walking his own tightrope. The slaves that he was writing to would often be exploited by their masters. There would not be just rewards for all. That is often true of our work. Those above us may exploit us or treat us unjustly. Those who cheat are not always caught, in fact they often get promotion. Those who are honest and quiet often do not get the rewards they are due. Those who make a stand on their Christian faith will often be persecuted.

A man who worked in a sales office became a Christian and felt under God that he could no longer make fraudulent expenses claims. However, this meant that the corruption among his fellow workers would come to light. He faced threats, isolation and eventually the sack for being honest.

In the light of all of this, there is justice. Those who may not get justice fully in this life need to know that 'you will receive an inheritance from the Lord as a reward' (v24). Those who do wrong will have to bear the consequences (v25), for God does not show favouritism.

However, that simply reinforces our responsibility now. Paul turns from the slaves to the masters, those who have power in our world (4:1). The implications of the future for the present are quite clear. Those who have power have responsibility to use it justly and well. It should not be under-estimated just how significant these words are. In Paul's world to talk of a master's responsibilities to slaves would be incredible, and to talk of justice in the context of slavery would to most people sound ludicrous. But that is what holiness requires.

Christians work in fallen structures. We need to accept that, and get on with it, being salt and light. Yet to be holy is to work to redeem the structures, that is working for structures to be improved.

In the chapel in the north east of England where I grew up, there was quite an odd thing at the front of the church. Alongside the expected cross, organ, pulpit and communion table there was a large banner which belonged to the National Union of Mineworkers. It was in the chapel as testimony to the Christians who had been influential in the rise of trade unions, fighting for justice at work. These Christians took holiness at work seriously. It was not just about working well down the coal pit, it was about being concerned with health and safety, fair wages and life outside work. In the same chapels, some of the bosses worshipped. To be holy at work was to be concerned for the same issues, and so to use their power and influence wisely and compassionately over others.

Those of us as Christians who hold power and influence need to use it under the Lordship of Christ, for we have a master in heaven who will one day hold us accountable.

Study and action

One book to read: J. Drane, *Work and Society* (Lion: Oxford, 1994).

One outline for discussion:
1. Ronald Sider writes, 'The values of our affluent society seep slowly and subtlely into our hearts and minds – the only way to defy them is to immerse ourselves deeply in Christian fellowship.' How can your local Christian fellowship help you at work?
2. What does your work mean to you?
3. What are your main motives in work?
4. How can your local fellowship support those who are out of work?

One question for yourself: The J. B. Phillips translation of Romans 12:2 is 'Don't let the world around you squeeze you into its own mould – instead let God remould you.' Are you being squeezed at work and how can you let God remould your attitude to work?

One action to take: Make contact with other Christians at your place of work. Perhaps advertise a short weekly prayer meeting, or if one already exists go along to it!

10

HOLIDAYS OR HOLYDAYS?

Holidays are big business. Each year 50 million holidays are taken in Britain, £3 billion is spent, and 9 million of us go overseas on package holidays. While not on holiday we can pore through the glossy magazines or watch the many travel programmes on television. The promise can be quite different from the reality. The broadcaster Cliff Michelmore has collected a number of quotations from various holiday brochures which did not come out as they were planned:

'If this is your first visit to our hotel you are welcome to it.'

'You will not be likely to forget quickly your experience with us.'

'If you wish for breakfast, lift the telephone, ask for room service, and this will be enough for you to bring your food up.'

'On gala nights, the chef throws his best dishes, and all water used in cooking has been passed by the manager personally.'

The pictures of secluded beaches, happy children, lovers walking arm in arm are nevertheless attractive, especially in the 'busy-ness' and pressure of life. The demands of young children, the demands of older children, families spread out over distances, the expectations of employers, longer and longer hours at work extended by commuting time, and the pressures of achievement and money all add to the longing to get away.

However, we can also easily feel guilty about it all. We can feel that there is something wrong in having time to ourselves. If we find our identity in our work it might be difficult for us to stop. If we are under debt or money pressures we might want to do more work to earn more money. If we are caring for others we may feel that we can never take time off to care for ourselves.

To be honest the church often makes it worse, encouraging people to spend every spare moment at this meeting or that meeting. The Archbishop of Canterbury recently spoke about a poster outside a church, which like the holiday adverts had got it slightly wrong. It said, 'Don't let worry kill you, let the church help.' The responsibilities that many of us stack up mean that we are often out at meetings at the church, catching up with work, and caring for others.

Often within our Christian tradition, to be holy is to do more and more. More time looking after others. More time working for the church. More time doing good works. It is as if our holiness increases with the depth of the bags under our eyes. I often get to the point of simply wanting to cry out that I just want a rest. Where do we get rest? We find rest in Jesus and the following passage speaks of that:

[28]'Come to me, all you who are weary and burdened, and I will give you rest. [29]Take my yoke upon you and learn from me, for I am gentle and humble in heart, and you will find rest for your souls. [30]For my yoke is easy and my burden is light.'

12 At that time Jesus went through the cornfields on the Sabbath. His disciples were hungry and began to pick some ears of corn and eat them. [2]When the Pharisees saw this, they said to him, 'Look! Your disciples are doing what is unlawful on the Sabbath.' [3]He answered, 'Haven't you read what David did when he and his companions were hungry? [4]He entered the house of God, and he and his companions ate the consecrated bread – which was not lawful for them to do, but only for the priests. [5]Or haven't you read in the Law that on the Sabbath the priests in the temple desecrate the day and yet are innocent? [6]I tell you that one greater than the temple is here. [7]If you had known what these words mean, "I desire mercy, not sacrifice," you would not have condemned the innocent. [8]For the Son of Man is Lord of the Sabbath.'

[9]Going on from that place, he went into their synagogue, [10]and a man with a shrivelled hand was there. Looking for a reason to accuse Jesus, they asked him, 'Is it lawful to heal on the Sabbath?' [11]He said to them, 'If any of you has a sheep and it falls into a pit on the Sabbath, will you not take hold of it and lift it out? [12]How much more valuable is a human being than a sheep! Therefore it is lawful to do good on the Sabbath.' [13]Then he said to the man, 'Stretch out your hand.' So he stretched it out and it was completely restored, just as sound as the other. [14]But the Pharisees went out and plotted how they might kill Jesus.

(Matthew 11:28–12:14)

Holiness recognises a time of rest

Many of us go through life not thinking that we need a rest or a holiday. Sometimes it creeps up on us or through ill health we are finally forced to recognise our needs.

A few years ago I was invited with a number of other church leaders to go to Seoul in South Korea to look at the amazing growth of the Church there. We were hosted by a Methodist Church which in 1970 had 100 members, and which had grown to 50,000 at the time of our visit. As you can imagine it was a thrilling time. Not only did we want to learn what God was doing, we wanted to make the most of being in another country and culture.

The days were long and while I was there I became ill with a virus. I only had two weeks there so instead of resting I carried on. When I returned to the UK I felt worse. Part of me felt I needed a rest, but I had come back at a busy time for the church, my desk was full, and people needed to be visited. I was also excited at what I had seen in Korea and secretly felt that I had actually been on a type of holiday for the past two weeks.

Instead of resting I continued with work. For almost the next year I was unable to get rid of the effects of the virus. I became weaker and picked up every other virus that seemed to be going around. Eventually I became so ill that I was signed off work for two months, but I guess it was yet another year before I was back at full strength. I needed to recognise that I needed rest. Eventually my health gave way and I had to have much longer off than if I had taken rest when I first came back to the UK.

It is at times very difficult for us to admit that we have a need. But Jesus gives us an invitation. It is to 'all you who are weary and burdened'(v28). Now this is not just for those who need a short break. The word 'weary' signifies a continuing state. It is for those who are weary searching for truth and for the relief of a troubled conscience. It is for those who are weary with a sense of futility and frustration in life.

In addition to the weary are those who are heavily burdened. Again it has the sense of a continuous state. Jesus may be referring here to the heavy load that religion can put upon people. Later in the Gospel, Matthew refers to Jesus criticising teachers and Pharisees because 'they tie up heavy loads and put them on other people's shoulders but they themselves are not willing to lift a finger to move them' (Mt 23:4). I remember once having a back problem and so asking two students to carry some heavy tables. I stood there not sure what to do as my two friends struggled with the heavy load I had placed upon them.

Whatever specifically Jesus is referring to, there is a deeper principle here. Whether it be the frustration of life, the burdens of religion, the sorrows of life, fear, or too many pressures, the first step in achieving rest is acknowledging our need. Are we prepared to acknowledge that we are weary and burdened? Too often we are too proud to recognise our need. We say, 'I'm all right, but you have a rest if you need it.' Yet Jesus is asking us personally.

2. Holiness receives a time of rest

Holidays are often a time of receiving. For some who care for others, it is especially the time when they can have their meals cooked for them. The rest that Jesus talks about is not something we earn, or something we can work for, or something we deserve, or something we can save up for. It is a gift.

He says, 'I will give you' (v28). Jesus may be echoing Jeremiah 6:16 where rest is the offer of God, or Isaiah 40:27–31 where God offers strength to the weary. But the point is that here it is Jesus who is offering the rest. It is a free gift, but there needs to be a response if that rest is going to be real in your life. We need to 'take' (v29) and that for a lot of us is very difficult. We feel that in our relationship with God we should not receive anything until we deserve it. If I do a lot of good works then I will deserve rest. If I pray a lot then I deserve rest. Nothing could be further from the promise that God gives us. He offers a gift which we are invited to simply take.

Some of my colleagues at church are leaders of a discipling programme called Walk to Emmaus. It takes place as a weekend retreat and people receive teaching on what it means to be disciples. As well as good teaching, it also creates an atmosphere where people learn to receive. Those who have been on previous weekends come back to support and serve those who are on the weekend for the first time. People have to receive this support and service and this helps them to receive from Jesus.

3. Holiness is refreshed by a time of rest

Holidays are a time of refreshment. Someone once wrote, 'A good holiday makes you feel good enough to return to work – and so poor that you're forced to.'

When Jesus says, 'I will give you rest,' he is meaning, 'I will refresh you.' This does not mean 'stop doing anything at all'.

George Bernard Shaw once said, 'A perpetual holiday is a good working definition of hell.' To be a disciple of Jesus is to live a roller-coaster life, giving oneself for others. But as you give of yourself then Jesus gives himself to you.

The refreshing comes from learning from him. He is inviting people to follow him, to serve him, and the taking of the yoke means submission to authority, but an authority that is kindly and not a burden.

The Bible commentator Leon Morris writes, 'Those who bear Christ's yoke know rest at the centre of their being . . . those who take Christ's yoke on them have rest, rest now and eternal rest in the hereafter.'[1] I am sure that I have equated holiness with endless activity because I have failed to fully grasp the meaning of justification by faith rather than by works. Those who trust in Jesus Christ do not have to endlessly try and justify themselves before God; God justifies them.

The rest Jesus speaks about involves a time of recognising need, a time for receiving and a time of refreshment. But how does it happen?

4. Holiness means being very practical about a time of rest

In biblical terms it happens in a very practical way and very personal way. We need to note here the way that these words of Jesus are linked to the following account of his relation to the Sabbath, the day of rest (Mt 12:1–14).

L. T. Johnson writes, 'The commandment that above all defined Jews in society was the Sabbath observance, which was regarded as participation in God's own Sabbath rest; here learning from Jesus brings rest for the soul.'[2] The controversy over the use and meaning of the Sabbath follows on from Jesus' words. The Pharisees, who criticised the disciples for picking corn and eating it, had the wrong idea of the Sabbath. Instead of a day of rest the regulations surrounding the Sabbath were being used as a heavy burden. In healing the man with the shrivelled hand in the synagogue, Jesus directly challenges these Pharisees to think again. The Sabbath should be a time of honouring God, of doing good, of refreshment and healing, and of meeting people's needs. The principle behind it is the biblical command for rest, that is the importance of a break to the normal work of life, and the opportunity to do something different.

Jesus' claim to be Lord of the Sabbath, coupled with his words about rest are a direct claim to divinity. They also link together the spiritual refreshment that Jesus offers with the very practical avenue of having a break from the normal. That is to have a time to recognise need, receive and be refreshed. This applies not just to the spiritual part of us, but to the physical and emotional. The Sabbath principle for Christians is not just about making space to worship and fellowship with other Christians, it is about making space to be refreshed in all aspects of our God-given humanity. This is a biblical advert for holidays and days off. R. T. France has written that the Sabbath was a gift of God to make Israel more holy – to give time and space for the people to remember God's work of creation, his special relationship with them and the joys of the world to come.

It is very easy as a minister to become a Pharisee. I often find myself stressing the importance of worship, the prayer meeting, the Bible studies, the church working party, the committees, the special events with special speakers, the need for volunteers for the coffee rota and the need for children's workers. Sometimes the notices are as long as the sermon. And I can doubt the holiness of people very severely if they do not turn up to the events I have planned. All these things are important, but rest is also important. A leader of our neighbouring churches said to me the other day that if he sees his people once at worship on Sunday and one time during the week then he is satisfied. The rest of the time he encourages them to work, witness and enjoy.

Working in a job with irregular hours I have found that I must plan ahead in great detail. My wife and I plan days off up to a year ahead. If we didn't do that then our diaries would become so full that we would never see each other. We make sure that we put aside a proportion of our income for holidays. I have found a small retreat house half an hour from my home which is a place for rest and prayer. We make sure we go to movies and spend time with the children. I have had to learn from my wife and children how holy that time is – and I still have a lot to learn.

However many holidays and days off we take, the personal aspect remains. He is Lord of the Sabbath, the Lord of rest. He invites me to recognise my needs and to come to him.

We need to ask the following questions:

- Am I making time and space to worship and fellowship with other Christians?
- Am I making time and space to be with family and friends?
- Am I making time for myself for leisure and refreshment?

The holy answer to all those questions is 'yes'.

Study and action

One book to read: G. MacDonald, *Ordering Your Private World* (Highland Books: 1993).

One outline for discussion:
1. What's your favourite holiday and why?
2. How can our local fellowship encourage those who are weary and burdened to have rest?
3. Do you find rest easy to take or not?
4. Share times when God has refreshed you – in worship, on retreat or on holiday.

One question for yourself: What needs do I have before God?

One thing to do: Make a time chart of a number of typical weeks. Highlight in different marker pens the following:

a) time with friends and family

b) work

c) time spent at church

d) time to yourself for rest and relaxation

e) time in prayer and Bible study alone

Share with a friend what changes you would like to make to your use of time.

Notes

1. Leon Morris, *Matthew* (IVP: Leicester, 1995), p. 297.
2. Quoted by Leon Morris, *Ibid.*, p. 295.

PART 3
Holiness and the World

11

HOLY PROVOCATION

What extraordinary things happen on holiday! Not so long ago, a rather frail old lady from the English village of St Mary Meade was not too well and so was sent on a Caribbean holiday by her nephew Raymond. It just so happened that her visit coincided with a series of murders on the holiday island and she was able to solve the mystery.

I was on holiday myself as I watched that particular episode of BBC TV's *Miss Marple*, adapted from the Agatha Christie murder mysteries. It did strike me as rather odd that wherever this woman went in the world murders seemed to happen! In fact, an impartial observer may conclude that Miss Marple herself is the only common thing in a whole series of murders and therefore must ask the question whether she herself is a very clever serial killer. However, such speculation aside, Miss Marple always rises to the task of helping the police, even on holiday.

Most of us resent taking our work on holiday. We laugh at the nuclear scientist who put a note on his door during his vacation reading 'Gone Fission'. We rightly squirm at the missionary, J. Ockenga, of whom it is said that he took a suitcase full of theological textbooks on his honeymoon! In the last chapter I suggested the holy imperative of rest, and some practical issues from that. We now need to move on to a different discussion and let me ask whether we are living the Christian life as a constant holiday away from the world.

In Acts 17, Paul seemed to be on holiday in Athens. In the past few months he had had a somewhat difficult time. He had disagreed and gone his separate way with his long time friend and mission partner, Barnabas (Acts 15:36–41). Sent to Macedonia by a direct intervention of the Holy Spirit, he had been verbally abused, arrested, stripped, severely flogged and imprisoned in Philippi. He had then caused a riot in Thessolonica and had to leave to avoid a mob, who eventually followed him to Berea. In order to avoid trouble at Berea, Paul was 'sent' to Athens while his helpers, Silas and Timothy stayed. Reading between the lines it almost seems that Silas and Timothy felt it was safer all round for them to follow up the converts at Berea, while Paul had an enforced rest. The trouble was that Paul liked to work on holiday!

[16]While Paul was waiting for them in Athens, he was greatly distressed to see that the city was full of idols. [17]So he reasoned in the synagogue with the Jews and the God-fearing Greeks, as well as in the market-place day by day with those who happened to be there. [18]A group of Epicurean and Stoic philosophers began to dispute with him. Some of them asked, 'What is this babbler trying to say?' Others remarked, 'He seems to be advocating foreign gods.' They said this because Paul was preaching the good news about Jesus and the resurrection. [19]Then they took him and brought him to a meeting of the Areopagus, where they said to him, 'May we know what this new teaching is that you are presenting? [20]You are bringing some strange ideas to our ears, and we want to know what they mean.' [21](All the Athenians and the foreigners who lived there spent their time doing nothing but talking about and listening to the latest ideas.)

[22]Paul then stood up in the meeting of the Areopagus and said: 'People of Athens! I see that in every way you are very religious. [23]For as I walked around and looked carefully at your objects of worship, I even found an altar with this inscription: TO AN

UNKNOWN GOD. Now what you worship as something unknown I am going to proclaim to you.

24"The God who made the world and everything in it is the Lord of heaven and earth and does not live in temples built by hands. 25And he is not served by human hands, as if he needed anything, because he himself gives all life and breath and everything else. 26From one man he made all the nations, that they should inhabit the whole earth; and he determined the times set for them and the exact places where they should live. 27God did this so that they would seek him and perhaps reach out for him and find him, though he is not far from each one of us. 28"For in him we live and move and have our being." As some of your own poets have said, "We are his offspring."

29"Therefore since we are God's offspring, we should not think that the divine being is like gold or silver or stone – an image made by human design and skill. 30In the past God overlooked such ignorance, but now he commands all people everywhere to repent. 31For he has set a day when he will judge the world with justice by the man he has appointed. He has given proof of this to everyone by raising him from the dead.'

32When they heard about the resurrection of the dead, some of them sneered, but others said, 'We want to hear you again on this subject.' 33At that, Paul left the Council. 34 Some of the people became followers of Paul and believed. Among them was Dionysius, a member of the Areopagus, also a woman named Damaris, and a number of others.

(Acts 17:16–34)

This is one of my favourite passages of the Bible. It shows how holiness affects everyday life.

1. A holy person is provoked by the world

At this time, although Athens was in decline it was still the region's intellectual metropolis. Imagine how a graduate of Tarsus and Jerusalem must have felt to be in Athens with nothing to do. A chance to look around the architecture and the sights such as the Parthenon. To go to the Agora, the market place, and to listen to the debates about art, literature and philosophy. Paul would have been tempted like any other tourist to 'do Athens'.

However, the main thing that struck him was not the beauty of the city nor the brilliance of the intellectual climate. It was the idolatry. Paul was 'greatly distressed to see that the city was full of idols' (v16). The words that Luke uses have the sense of the city being 'smothered' or 'swamped' with idols, or as one translation puts it, the city was a 'veritable forest of idols'. In fact a Roman satirist had written that it was 'easier to find a god there than a man' and Xenophon had characterised Athens as 'one great altar, one great sacrifice'. Everywhere you turned you would see temples, shrines, statues and altars to the likes of Athena, Apollo, Jupiter and Diana.

Paul's reaction was severe. The verb used to signify his distress can be used of a seizure or epileptic fit, and in fact the same word is used in the Old Testament to refer to God's reaction to idols. For example, the golden calf 'provoked the Lord God to anger' (Deut 9:7). Perhaps J. B. Phillips gives the best picture when he translates, 'His whole soul was revolted at the sight of a city given over to idolatry.'

Holiness has that effect. Growth in holiness deepens one's sensitivity to idolatry. Now of course, few of us walk down the street on holiday in the West and see golden statues of Jupiter. But an idol can be many things. It is a 'god substitute'which denies the reality of the Lord God and takes his rightful place for worship. We live in places which are still veritable forests of idols. The worshipping of greed, money, sex and power swamp our society.

Are we provoked by these things? I find myself asking searching questions. Does it distress me greatly that greed and injustice produce a situation where we are overfed while a major part of humanity starves? Am I revolted at the way that power is used to oppress people in sexism and racism? Does the worshipping of the gods of money and sex affect me at all? The trouble is that at times I am quite happy going ahead and building my little life, 'my' little church and my little spirituality, apathetic to what is going on around me.

Holiness is not about being on holiday from the world. It is not about living a life so cocooned from the world that it never affects us. Time after time in the Gospels Jesus is deeply affected by what he sees. At the death of Lazarus he weeps (Jn 11:35), at seeing Jerusalem he weeps (Lk 19:41) and as he saw the crowds of people lost and helpless he felt compassion (Mt 9:36). The word used for compassion here is the strongest word in the Greek language for pity. It means a stomach-churning or gut-wrenching feeling.

I have rarely come anywhere near that compassion. I remember holding back tears seeing the starving in Ethiopia on the television in the 1980s. I cried when at the end of Richard Attenborough's movie *Cry Freedom* there was what seemed to be a never-ending list of black people who had died in South African police custody. I cried during a church mission when people seemed so indifferent to the message of Jesus. But these instances have been rare.

A holy person should be affected by the idols of the world. The story is told of the missionary Henry Martyn engaged in translation work in India. He had dinner with some Muslim friends and during the course of the evening, one of his friends made a remark about Jesus kneeling at Mohammed's feet. Martyn became quite distressed and left. Later he was asked why. He replied that what had distressed him was that Jesus was not being acknowledged as rightful Lord. He said, 'I would not endure existence if Jesus was not glorified, it would be hell to me.'

2. A holy person is involved with the world

Paul's distress in Athens led to action. One of the key words is simply 'so'. As a result of his distress he began to 'reason in the synagogue' (v17) which was his usual practice when he arrived at a place. But he also engaged with those 'in the market place day by day' (v17). The market place or Agora was the centre of public life and Paul became involved there.

Paul's holiness did not mean that he simply threw his hands up in horror at a city of idols – it motivated him into getting involved. Within the New Testament there are many motives given for mission and evangelism such as recognising the love of the missionary God, hearing the great commission of Jesus to his disciples, and being prompted by the Holy Spirit. Here Paul is provoked by the world into mission.

In the market place he met and began to debate with a group of Epicurean and Stoic philosophers. They were the intellectuals of the place. For the Epicureans, god was remote, the world was due to chance collisions and pleasure was to be sought as a primary objective. The Stoics were pantheists, seeing god and the world as one and having a fatalism about all things.

Paul's reception was mixed. Some thought he was off his head. He's a 'babbler' or parrot they said. 'What is he trying to say?' Others seemed dismissive, accusing him of advocating foreign gods. But others invited him to the Areopagus, the main debating arena in town. It was only because Paul was in the Agora that he was invited to the Areopagus. It was only because he was committed to getting involved at the heart of everyday life that he was allowed to speak later at the influential opportunity. To use a well-worn but nevertheless important phrase he met people where they were, not where he wanted them to be.

I once received an invitation to speak at a philosophy club on the origin of the universe, with the express qualification that I should not 'bring God into it'. I was very busy at the time and wondered whether this was a good evangelistic opportunity. Nevertheless I went and found the group to be all atheists. I talked science all evening without any mention of God. A few weeks later I received another invitation to come back and this time to talk about God 'without bringing religion into it'. The third invitation was to come back and talk about Jesus. I only got the third invitation because they trusted me. As I talked about Jesus, some who had been intrigued by the intellectual discussion became cold. Others were warm in their response. I wish I could say that many became Christians that night. That did not happen and soon I went to work in another part of the country. Whether they responded or not, I do believe that seeds were sown.

It was quite a risk for Paul to go to the Areopagus. It would be only human to worry about the intellectual power of those who would question him. Although some had invited him because they honestly wanted to know more, others would simply want to humiliate him. He also risked a more subtle danger. It was the danger of trivialising the gospel. Luke records that those who were there 'spent their time doing nothing but talking about and listening to the latest ideas' (v21) or as another translation puts it, 'spent their time in useless discussion'! Paul ran the risk of presenting the gospel alongside useless and trendy philosophies and some would say that was out of the question.

Yet Paul knew that to share the good news means becoming vulnerable. Churches today need to learn that. I often feel that we would have adopted the mission strategy of setting up a church building in Athens and inviting people onto our territory to be bamboozled by songs they did not know, shorthand theology they could not understand and fifteen books of songs and liturgy. And we would not allow them to ask questions!

I find that God uses me most powerfully with those who are not Christians when I am at my most vulnerable. If asked to speak about the Christian faith I prefer to do so outside church buildings and with a good amount of time for questions. Paul went to people so that they could come to Jesus. He became involved with people and involved in their world. Part of that involvement was the way he presented the gospel. He had observed their worship (v23), studied their poets (v28) and from the theological points of his talk seemed to understand very well both Epicurean and Stoic philosophy.

It is a misleading understanding of holiness that over-emphasises a separation between the disciple and the world. Some argue that there are some movies which should not 'be viewed by Christians' and some music which is 'of the devil'. Pubs and nightclubs should not be visited. The fear is that the holy person will be contaminated by the world. Holiness is not like that. It is about being involved in order to witness and redeem. We have recently planted a new congregation in a pub in the city centre of Liverpool. The worship happens with the pub open, the jukebox competing with the worship band, and the leaders not knowing who is going to be in the congregation.

Of course, we run the risk of temptations and the subtle pressure of sub-Christian lifestyles and thoughtforms in all that we do. The trouble is that such arguments can be used for Christians to retreat from the world and God's mission of evangelism. In a Christian sub-culture where there are so many Christian meetings to go to, so many Christian tapes to listen to and books to read, we need to be careful not to retreat from the world. This Christian sub-culture can be safe and secure.

From that safety and security, it is very easy to be holy in such a way that we throw our hands up in self-righteous horror at what the world is doing. A woman who had no contact with the church began to come to our church, but left after a few months. I visited and asked her why. She said simply, 'I feel I am being judged by you people.' An occupational hazard of Christians is to do that. Within my own denomination, Methodism, in times past if a person drank alcohol then they would be looked down upon. In some churches if people do not dress appropriately, if they do not speak in the right way, if they ask too many questions then they are looked down upon.

The gospel, however, starts where people are, not where we want them to end up. Peter was a friend of mine at university who spoke in such a way that at least one word every sentence would need to be bleeped out! He became a Christian and came along to the CU prayer meeting where he talked to his new-found Father in a very natural way. The trouble was that the rest of us 'holy' Christians had never heard prayers interspersed with so many swear words! What was important at that time was that Peter prayed; the Holy Spirit would deal with his language as time went on.

The supreme example of a holy person involved in the world was of course Jesus. He was the 'friend of sinners', eating and sharing with a wide range of people. He was criticised by the religious, but he shared God's love with all.

To be holy is a motive for evangelism. It is to ask, where is our Agora or Areopagus? Where is the place where people are at the centre of community? If it is the pub, the club or the café, then are we there also? We need to affirm that part of the life of holiness is to be part of the parents' association, the Amnesty International meeting and the hockey club. Are we aware of the discussions and debates which shape thinking in our society, whether they are raised by films, music, sport, television soaps or magazines?

3. A holy person proclaims to the world

It is hard to imagine any less receptive or more scornful an audience than the one Paul would have addressed when he got to the Areopagus. He begins gently, sharing common ground by referring to the inscription he has seen, 'To an unknown God' (v23). However, this is not where he ends.

Paul takes the opportunity boldly by stating that 'I am going to proclaim to you' that God can be known. His proclamation of God as creator of the universe (v24), sustainer of life (v25), ruler of all nations (v26) and the one who is close to us (v27) challenges the Epicureans' belief that God was remote and the Stoics' belief that God was part of the universe. His argument is that on the basis of this God who can be known, idolatry just does not make sense. Yet Paul goes even further. Life in this world is not to be pursued only for pleasure, or viewed as if nothing will change. For all people are called to repent in the light of God's coming judgement. The evidence for this is to be found in Jesus and the resurrection. Paul is not afraid, even in this audience, to proclaim the good news about Jesus and what our response should be. Sometimes those who take involvement in the world seriously forget that there is a distinctive Christian proclamation which is divisive. In the words of David Watson, some of us are happier making the prodigal son more comfortable in the pigsty rather than calling him back to the father.

The good news of Jesus comes with a call to repentance. This means the call to change your mind and change your life and live in God's way. Christians can be positive about many things in this world, but without the call to repentance both evangelism and social action can be shallow.

The reaction was mixed. Some mocked and sneered. They probably questioned Paul's intellect or disparaged his appearance. 'He's so simplistic, life is more complicated than that'; 'Does he not know any basic philosophy?' 'How arrogant to go on like that!' However, some asked to hear more and others even believed (vv32–34).

Some older commentaries on this passage argue that Paul's mission here was a failure. They point out that only a few believed. In addition, they put together the fact that Luke records that Paul visited Corinth next (Acts 18:1–17) with Paul's claim in 1 Corinthians 2:1–5 that when he visited Corinth he came not with wisdom but preaching 'Jesus Christ and him crucified'. So the argument goes, after Paul's failure he saw that trying to debate in the way he had done in Athens was wrong. When he arrived at Corinth he changed his message and simply preached the cross. Therefore we should not get involved with the wisdom of the world but simply preach the 'old simple gospel'.

Such an argument is attractive but misleading. First, the fact is that Paul did make converts at Athens. We are not sure just how long Paul stayed there or how this new Christian community developed. There are claims that some of the names mentioned in 17:34 became significant leaders of the church. Second, Paul cannot be accused of not calling for repentance in the most direct way. It is true that in Luke's account there is no mention of the cross but that is not to say that this is all that Paul said both in the Areopagus and outside. Third, there is an important principle that Paul applies and communicates the same gospel message in a multitude of ways in the New Testament, depending on the people and context he is addressing.

The proclamation of the gospel in Romans is a logical step by step telling of the good news of Jesus against an often legal background. The good news of Jesus is presented in Colossians as the supremacy of Christ in all things. In Ephesians Paul gets so excited that the good news is presented in the context of God's plan for the whole universe. As the one gospel impacts different cultures, places, times and peoples so Christians are called under the Holy Spirit to proclaim the good news in a way that allows people to hear it in ways that makes sense.

I feel constantly challenged by this. It is more than simply knowing the basic message or calling for repentance. Our involvement in the world should lead to opportunities to speak, but also a better understanding of how to speak. The language and images that I use as I preach on Sunday have to work in the office or on the factory floor. What does the message of Jesus say to those situations? No one should misunderstand the time and effort that is involved in this, or indeed the cost of rejection or abuse.

The missionary God, out of compassion for his people, became involved in our world as a human being, living and proclaiming the message of his love for us, ultimately dying our death on the cross. The missionary pioneer, C. T. Studd said, 'If Jesus Christ is God and died for me, then no sacrifice is too great for him.' I am humbled each time I hear those words. Is the Christian life a perpetual holiday? Am I continually receiving in a kind of spiritual Disneyland while the world goes on outside? Miss Marple could have thought of many excuses for why she should not get involved with the murders on her Caribbean holiday. After all, she was very old, she had done her bit many times before, she did not have a gun to protect herself, and she was on holiday. But the need was there and she responded.

Study and action

One book to read: J. R.W. Stott, *New Issues Facing Christians Today* (Marshall Pickering: London, 1998).

One outline for discussion:
1. What are the hardest things in trying to share our faith?
2. How as a local fellowship can we encourage and support one another in sharing our faith?
3. What provokes you about the world?
4. In evangelistic events that you have held or that you have been to, who are the most vulnerable – those who are Christians or those who are not?

One question for yourself: Where does God want you to be involved?

One action to take: Each day pray for opportunities to share your faith.

12

HOLY OZONE LAYER

If the ozone layer were at ground level it would be as thin as a sheet of paper. However, high in the atmosphere this layer of gas expands and protects the surface of the earth very well from ultraviolet radiation. This form of radiation provides sun worshippers with tanned skin. The ozone layer lets through enough ultraviolet to provide the tanned bodies of *Baywatch*. Yet too much ultraviolet means that skin burns and skin cancer appears. Some years ago scientists began to notice a depletion in the ozone layer above the South Pole. The cause of this was the action of certain gases which we were putting into the atmosphere every time we used an aerosol for our hair or trashed a fridge. Stung by public concern, governments and manufacturing companies have slowly reduced the levels of these destructive gases, although there is still a long way to go.

Should Christians be interested in such a thing? Should it be included in a book on holiness? Apart from the fact that the pun gives a neat chapter heading, does holiness make a difference to the environment? Very few Christians would say that the environment was unimportant, but few would say it is of central importance to the holy life. Once again, that view of holiness which sees things in an individualistic and 'other worldly' way surfaces. Surely, people say, holiness is about our inward life. Yes, it might be about caring for other people but not the environment. You need to get priorities right.

In the past few years, I have heard the following arguments used by Christian people against involvement in environmental concerns. Indeed, I have to admit that I have used them myself:

- What we are about as Christians is simply saving souls.
- This world is destined to be burned up in God's judgement, so it is basically a lost cause.
- A lot of the people who are into the environment are people who are also into New Age, paganism, Mother Earth and all that sort of thing – and we don't want to get involved with people like that.
- We are given control of everything, so we are able to do with the world what we want.
- This material world is of little importance compared to the 'spiritual world' of heaven.

Such arguments have led many Christians to dismiss the importance of the environment. In addition, there are pressures which we share with those in the industrialised West whether they are Christians or not. As environmental changes increasingly impact the poor in the two-thirds world, we are often cocooned from any feeling of danger by our comfortable lifestyle. Many of us have grown up in a culture which divorces us from the natural world, and we have the belief that all-powerful science will save us from any mess we make – whether it be providing new sources of energy or even new planets to travel to when we have finished with this one. The scientific data on the environment is often hard to understand and it is even more difficult sometimes to know what to do. Finally, we have to acknowledge the difference between concern and making changes to our lifestyle that will cause some sacrifice.

A classic way to inspire environmental action is to list the horrendous state that the world is in, in terms of the wasting of global resources in the face of increasing population, the loss of biodiversity, global pollution of the land, atmosphere and the sea, global warming and the hole in the ozone layer above the North and South Poles. I have followed this way elsewhere.[1] The line of this argument is to see the problems we have and how they threaten our world, and to do something about it.

The trouble that I have with this view is that it can be quite selfish. The world's in such a bad state, we'd better do something about it or we will die! Christians need to be informed of such things, but they are not our only or indeed prime motive for environmental action. We are not about knee-jerk reactions because we are worried about our own survival for the future. We need to learn to care for the environment because of the Bible's doctrine of creation.

We therefore need to turn the following passage:

[26]Then God said, 'Let us make human beings in our image, in our likeness, and let them rule over the fish of the sea and the birds of the air, over the livestock, over all the earth, and over all the creatures that move along the ground.'

[27]So God created human beings in his own image,
in the image of God he created them;
male and female he created them.

[28]God blessed them and said to them, 'Be fruitful and increase in number; fill the earth and subdue it. Rule over the fish of the sea and the birds of the air and over every living creature that moves on the ground.'

[29]Then God said, 'I give you every seed-bearing plant on the face of the whole earth and every tree that has fruit with seed in it. They will be yours for food. [30]And to all the beasts of the earth and all the birds of the air and all the creatures that move on the ground – everything that has the breath of life in it – I give every green plant for food.' And it was so.

[31]God saw all that he had made, and it was very good. And there was evening, and there was morning – the sixth day.

2 Thus the heavens and the earth were completed in all their vast array. [2]By the seventh day God had finished the work he had been doing; so on the seventh day he rested from all his work. [3]And God blessed the seventh day and made it holy, because on it he rested from all the work of creating that he had done.

[4]This is the account of the heavens and the earth when they were created.

When the Lord God made the earth and the heavens – [5]and no shrub of the field had yet appeared on the earth and no plant of the field had yet sprung up, for the Lord God had not sent rain on the earth and there was no-one to work the ground, [6]but streams came up from the earth and watered the whole surface of the ground – [7]the Lord God formed a man from the dust of the ground and breathed into his nostrils the breath of life, and the man became a living being.

[8]Now the Lord God had planted a garden in the east, in Eden; and there he put the man he had formed. [9]And the Lord God made all kinds of trees grow out of the ground – trees that were pleasing to the eye and good for food. In the middle of the garden were the tree of life and the tree of knowledge of good and evil.

[10]A river watering the garden flowed from Eden; from there it was separated into four headwaters. [11]The name of the first is the Pishon; it winds through the entire land of Havilah, where there is gold. [12](The gold of that land is good; aromatic resin and onyx are also there.) The name of the second river is the Gihon; it winds through the entire land of Cush. [14]The name of the third river is the Tigris; it runs along the east side of Asshur. And the fourth river is the Euphrates.

[15]The Lord God took the man and put him in the Garden of Eden to work it and take care of it. [16]And the Lord God commanded the man, 'You are free to eat from any tree in the garden; [17]but you must not eat from the tree of the knowledge of good and evil, for when you eat of it you will surely die.'

(Genesis 1:26–2:17)

1. Holy creation

The trouble with many of us is that we have never fully understood the Bible's teaching on creation. For some years when I turned to these Genesis passages I was obsessed with questions over whether they tell of a creation a few thousand years ago or billions of years ago, or whether evolution is compatible with the biblical account. Some Christians argue strongly that Genesis is a literal scientific account of a creation over six days and that evolution is totally incompatible with it. Some then go further and claim that belief in evolution is one of the main reasons for the decline of morality and holiness within society, due to the fact that it says that men and women are no different from animals. Other Christians, equally committed to the authority of the Bible, claim that these passages are not a literal scientific account and that evolution may be God's way of creating.

I am not concerned in this book over the question of the truth of either of these positions, since these are arguments that I have explored elsewhere. However, I do want to point out a danger and what for me is an increasing frustration. That is that the evolution issue and the dating of the early chapters in Genesis have often clouded our minds to the clear truths of creation in the Bible. This has meant confusion and a lack of holiness in our lifestyle.

The first thing that the Bible says and reiterates time after time is that the whole universe is creation, that is it owes its origin and continued existence to the sovereign will of God. Look, for example, at the repeated use of 'all' in the above chapter – we are left in no doubt that the whole of the natural world, whether heavens, earth, vegetation, animals or human beings was created by God.

The world is not ours to do with as we please, 'The earth is the Lord's, and everything in it' (Ps 24:1). The Lord is the creator of all things and the world is entirely dependent on him. Our holy perspective is that we value the world as God's creation, not because it is divine and we need to worship it, or even because we want to keep it so we will be selfishly all right. Furthermore, Christians are not simply concerned with the 'spiritual'. We do not believe that the material world is evil and worthless. It has been created by God, and whatever has gone wrong with the world through our fall from God's ways, the creation still has value.

My training was as a scientist. I was fortunate that my Christian faith grew with my interest in science and I was helped by many older scientists into understanding that science was a holy vocation just as important as preaching or evangelism. Those who study the universe, whether it be in the nature of the universe itself in cosmology, the fundamental laws in physics, the way that atoms and molecules interact together in chemistry, the nature of living things in biology, psychology and sociology, are all engaged in holy occupations. Those who use the creation in engineering and technology, those who care for the creation in gardening, refuse disposal and environmentalism are all doing holy work. For we are thinking God's thoughts after him and looking after his creation.

2. Holy keeping

God creates all things, and then gives us a distinctive role. Some biblical scholars point out the differences between two accounts of creation, one finishing at verse 3 of chapter 2 and the other beginning at verse 4. Whatever the arguments about their origin it is clear that there is a real difference in the style of the accounts. However, we sometimes make the mistake of looking at them in isolation. The Old Testament scholar Gerhard Von Rad pointed out that the two are in the Bible together and while recognising their differences we should also recognise that the two interact. No more so than in the role God gives to human beings.

In verse 26 of chapter 1 and again in verse 27 God makes human beings in his own image. Connected with that are three other things that are not shared by the rest of God's creation.

That is to 'rule over' (vv26, 28), to 'fill the earth' (v28) and to 'subdue it' (v28). Other translations have 'dominion' rather than 'rule'. To see what that means we need to read on to verse 15 of chapter 2 where this special relationship of God and human beings is amplified in the picture of a garden. 'The Lord God took the man and put him in the Garden of Eden to work it and take care of it' (2:15).

It seems to me that is a very helpful way of understanding God's giving of dominion. God gives human beings responsibility under him for this world. 'To work it and take care of it' can also be translated as 'to serve and keep it'. We are given responsibility for wise stewardship and use of the creation, but at the same time we must humbly take care of it. We must keep it. What does that mean?

While visiting another country I was once given use of another person's flat. He had left the country and for the two months I was there I had his flat. It was both a privilege and a responsibility. Unsure of exactly when he was returning I attempted to keep his flat in the best of condition. That did not mean that I did not use his pans for cooking, or sleep on the floor in case by some freak accident I broke his bed! I was able to use the flat, but he owned it.

To work and keep God's creation is to understand, use and care for it. From the passage you see important things about creation. Its goodness is emphasised time after time (1:31). We need to allow people to celebrate that goodness. It is a place of resources, not only food and water but mineral resources (2:12). We need to safeguard and make available all those resources which God has given us. It is a place of beauty, where trees are pleasing to the eye (2:9). It is a place of diversity with 'all kinds of trees' (2:9). Part of our keeping is to protect and value the biodiversity of the planet.

Human beings are created in the image of God. As God's representative, we are to act in a Godlike way. Throughout Genesis 1 and 2 God acts as a friend to creation, and so must we. Therefore to be holy as God is holy is to show care for God's creation. This has been reflected in a long Christian history of the linking together of biblical spirituality and appreciation and care for the natural world. From Francis of Assisi, through the Celtic Church to the biblical roots of the scientific revolution and on to the environmental movements of recent times, Christians have played a key role in caring for the planet. Such care, however, is not to be seen as simply maintaining the Garden of Eden and not doing anything. Under God we are asked to make the world a better place. We are to fill the earth and subdue it (1:28). Human beings have a God-given role to serve creation through action. Genesis 1 sees God as bringing order from chaos as part of his creative process. As stewards we are to make this world a better place through farming, science, architecture or medicine.

3. Holy action

At the end of the passage, God adds a command not to eat from the tree of knowledge of good and evil (2:17). As we read on that is exactly what Adam and Eve do, with severe consequences. Relationships are affected. Their relationship with God changes from intimacy to fear (3:8), their relationship with one another is broken and their relationship with creation is broken, shown by the expulsion from the Garden of Eden and the curse on the land (3:17–24).

This adds another dimension to caring for the earth. Because of our broken relationship with God we have not exercised dominion under him. Thinking of ourselves as lords of creation we have often used the earth for our own selfish purposes, abusing it and using resources recklessly. Christians share responsibility for this misuse, misunderstanding that dominion is to be exercised following the model of Jesus the servant. However, in this situation Christians can make a distinctive contribution to the environmental movement. Our holy action is to:

a) Repent

Before a holy God we need to acknowledge our sin and pledge ourselves to living differently. This does not just apply to sexual sin or jealousy but the way we are part of bigger structures that go against God's purposes. We cannot simply point the finger at others and fail to see our own responsibility. We need to confess that we have fallen short of God's purposes in being good stewards of the planet. We need to confess our part in the messing up of God's good creation both individually and corporately, and pledge ourselves to be good stewards. One day we will be judged for how we have cared for God's creation.

In multi-media worship or teaching we have shown images of pollution cut with images of the beauty of creation. Such images lead naturally to prayers of confession. We need to be specific about our sin, for God can use that confession in forgiving us and changing us.

b) Change our lifestyle

It is sometimes said that if only we knew what to do we would do it. To be holy is to understand what to do and do it. Ignorance is no excuse for doing nothing. There are many books, television programmes, leaflets written both by Christians and others which give clear guidance on how we might make our lifestyle more holy in this environmental context.

It is easy to start. Cut down on waste, recycle as much as possible, and reduce energy use either in heating or transport. We can begin at home and in our churches. I was introduced at one church with the words, 'Here is the man who inspired us to get our bin.' I had not the slightest idea what they were talking about, but I later found out that they had acted on a suggestion in a previous book that churches should recycle as much as possible. They had developed the idea and had provided recycling bins for the community on their premises.

Very simple things can be done such as switching off lights when not used, and this will also save money. Other things will involve spending time with others at home, at work or at church looking at these issues and making practical plans for the future. The book recommended at the end of this chapter gives specific suggestions for such action. Even small changes can have big effects.

c) Use our influence for change

We saw in chapter 3 that being holy is to act as salt and light in the world. The very changing of our lifestyle will act as a prophetic sign to others. Furthermore we need to use whatever influence we have in promoting environmental concerns. Our place of work is an obvious example and it can often be an individual taking the lead that makes a great difference. What about providing and looking after a recycling bin at the office?

On a more global scale, we need to put pressure on governments to change policy towards caring rather than exploiting the environment. Holiness is about getting involved in politics. Sometimes this is a messy business and we need to support especially those Christians who attempt to use their influence for change.

One aspect in particular needs to be addressed, that is the link between poverty and environment. The poor live on the most vulnerable land and are often the victims of the rich's exploitation of the environment. At the same time, in order to simply survive in the midst of poverty, people mess up the environment. The missiologist, Chris Sugden says, 'To protect the environment means addressing poverty and this will mean increasing poor people's share of world trade.'

d) Enjoy the environment

The new interest in paganism and nature worship may partly have developed because Christians have not led the way in celebrating God's good creation. Apart from harvest festivals, we have rarely brought creation into worship. We are not meant to worship creation, but creation itself can remind us of the goodness and power of God. To be holy is to take time and space to enjoy the environment, whether through science, gardening or simply getting out of our Western consumer bubble of technology and experiencing the natural world. For as we enjoy, we will see even more of the beauty of God's creation.

When I first began to work with my friend Rob Frost it was on one of his projects called *Pilgrims*. I found the idea quite simple and mind-blowing. Instead of praying indoors we prayed outdoors using our senses to inform our prayer. Whether in the countryside or in the urban setting, by simply looking around I have found my prayer life enhanced.

Study and action

One book to read: G. Prance, *The Earth under Threat: A Christian Perspective* (Wild Goose Publications, 1996).

One outline for discussion:
1. What do you enjoy about creation?
2. What can your local fellowship do to help the community care for creation?
3. What can your local fellowship do to be more environmentally friendly?
4. How can you bring enjoyment of creation and confession of our lack of care into worship?

One question for yourself: In daily life how can you enjoy and care for God's creation?

One action to take: Clean up a polluted area – that may be your garden, a local park or it may mean getting involved in a project nationally or overseas.

Notes

1. Rob Frost and David Wilkinson, *A New Start? Hopes and Dreams for the New Millennium* (Hodder Headline: London, 1999).

13

JUST HOLINESS?

Ally McBeal is one of the top US comedy shows, and has achieved cult status in many groups on this side of the Atlantic. Starring Calista Flockhart, aided by a surreal dancing baby, it is a story of one young woman's life in the midst of work and trying to form a lasting relationship with a man. She is also a lawyer, and although that is a feature of the show it is not the most important. Indeed, sometimes the law simply seems to be a vehicle for the relationships.

Of course it is not alone in that. Films that involve 'justice' such as *The Firm* with Tom Cruise or Sylvester Stallone proclaiming, 'I am the law' in *Judge Dredd*, will be remembered as much for Cruise's smile and Stallone blowing people away rather than the technical or philosophical points of justice. The theme of justice needs to be there but somehow is always in the background.

The connection between holiness and justice does not seem to be obvious, but is always there in the background in the Bible. Indeed, the root word for justice is linked to a number of others in the Bible, in particular righteousness. In both Hebrew and Greek the words belong together both linguistically and theologically and you will often find them interchangeable in English versions. In 1 Thessalonians 2:10 'justice/righteousness' is linked directly with holiness in conduct, and following the birth of Jesus the sincere devotion of Simeon is linked to his just ways (Lk 2:25).

Recently I was asked to speak at a Christian Union on the theme of justice. They told me to pick any Bible passage I liked to base the talk on. In a sense I could have replied, 'The whole Bible', but that would have taken too long to read before the talk! Justice is a constant theme throughout the Bible but the following passage gives us a stepping-off point into the rest of the Bible. It is part of the book of Revelation where John sees in a vision a song of praise to God:

> Great and marvellous are your deeds, Lord God Almighty.
> Just and true are your ways, King of the ages.
> ⁴Who will not fear you, O Lord, and bring glory to your name?
> For you alone are holy.
> All nations will come and worship before you, for your righteous
>   acts have been revealed.

(Revelation 15:3b-4)

1. The holy God is just

You notice that the God who is holy, acts in ways that are 'just and true'. For all ages, the Lord shows by his deeds that he is a holy and just God. His justice is often linked to truth, moral integrity and faithfulness (eg. Deut 9:5–6; 32:4; Is 45:19). This is an immediate reminder that God's holiness is not an arbitrary or culturally changing quality. He is the same for all ages and can be relied upon. It also means that in the creator of the universe there is an answer to the question of what is right or wrong. Great debate goes on concerning whether justice is simply culturally or politically dependent. Is there any eternal justice or is the law purely created by human beings?

The Bible is clear that at the heart of the universe is a holy God who is the basis of all justice. Of course in different cultures and in different times the working out of justice will take different forms, but we need to continually refer back to God's ways. That is why Blackstone's *Commentary on English Law* begins without embarrassment with an exposition of the Ten Commandments as the basis of law in a holy nation. What are God's ways of justice at work through the Bible?

a) A holy God punishes evil

A holy God cannot tolerate wrong (Hab 1:13). His justice leads to condemnation (Rom 3:5–8). There are some who so promote the love of God that they deny any sense of God's holiness being expressed in justice. They argue that a loving God will forgive all and all will go to heaven. It seems attractive in some ways, but is repugnant in others. I cannot see how God can look at the Holocaust, ethnic cleansing in Rwanda or Bosnia, or people dying of famine because of an unjust sharing of resources and say, 'Well it doesn't matter, boys will be boys.' God's holiness reminds us of his revulsion at our sin, and his promise of justice, whether in this life or beyond.

b) A holy God affirms the good

He blesses the home of the righteous (Prov 3:33) and 'executes justice for the oppressed' (Ps 147:7). Of course his blessing may not be in physical ways or even in this life, but there is reward and justice in heaven. One of the worst things a minister is sometimes asked to do is to judge a fancy dress competition for children! You actually want to give a prize to everybody including the child who dresses in a black bin liner in order to be Batman. Unfortunately you have to choose one winner. God rewards all that is good.

c) A holy God saves

God's holiness expresses itself in his acts of salvation. Following David's adultery with Bathsheba and his murder of her husband he asks, 'Save me from bloodguilt, O God, the God who saves me, and my tongue will sing of your righteousness/justice'

(Ps 51:14). This is an interesting passage for David has already acknowledged his guilt. Here he is relying on God's justice for forgiveness in the midst of condemnation. He was appealing to the faithfulness and integrity of God's promises in the covenant made with the people of Israel. God is just and holy in fulfilling his own generously promised salvation. So when Isaiah calls God a righteous God and Saviour (Is 45:21), he is meaning that because God is just, he is therefore a saviour. In some of our more formal services, part of our liturgy includes the following verse as an assurance of forgiveness, 'If we confess our sins, he is faithful and just and will forgive us our sins and cleanse us from all unrighteousness' (1 John 1:8–9). We can know we are forgiven because he is just.

d) A holy God gives righteousness to us

We saw in chapter 4 that God gives holiness as a gift. Here the image is of righteousness and Paul expresses what God does for those who trust in Christ, 'not having a righteousness of my own that comes from the law, but that which is through faith in Christ – the righteousness that comes from God and is by faith' (Phil 3:9). The other day I picked up my son from school. As we walked home it began to rain. My coat was big enough that he could shelter inside it as I wrapped it round both him and me. It did make me look like the first pregnant man in South Liverpool! That is what God does for us, giving us his righteousness in our need.

We see all these aspects of holiness in the Lord Jesus. He condemned sin and put before us the challenge of living a holy life. He affirmed the good, encouraging faith and mercy in a wide variety of people. Ultimately he gave his life for each one of us, to save us and impart his righteousness. In his legal images of the gospel Paul expresses it: 'God presented him as a sacrifice of atonement, through faith in his blood. He did this to demonstrate his justice, because in his forbearance he had left the sins committed beforehand unpunished – he did it to demonstrate his justice at the present time, so as to be just and the one who justifies those who have faith in Jesus' (Rom 3:25–26).

Imagine a judge sitting in court. Before her is a young man accused of a crime and found guilty. The law states a financial penalty but the young man is unable to pay it. The judge pronounces sentence for that is what the law requires. She then pays the fine herself – being true to justice but showing mercy by bearing the cost herself. The holy God is just and true in condemning sin but on the cross takes the punishment himself.

How do I receive this forgiveness and righteousness? Jesus told a story where a man goes to the temple and simply says, 'God be merciful to me a sinner' (Lk 18:13). It is this man who went home justified.

2. The holy God wants a people of justice

My children have selective hearing. At least that seems to be the only reason for an unusual phenomenon. When I say, 'Do you want some chocolate?' they hear clearly and respond quickly. When I say at exactly the same volume, 'Can you please tidy your bedroom,' they seem unable to hear at all! They know what they want to hear. The same is often true of me. I have selective hearing of the gospel, conditioned by the kind of churches I have been involved with and the assumptions we have received from other Christians.

For a long time in the West justice was not a key issue to many Christians. It was talked about but it was not as important as evangelism, worship and spiritual gifts, and prayer. Books on holiness would not mention it at all. It seemed to be only discussed in terms of eternal hell. Indeed, those Christians who were committed to working for justice in the here and now were often accused of not being true Christians at all. Things have changed now. Bible-believing Christians in the West have begun to hear again God's concern for justice. It needs to be said that we have been enormously helped in this by global

Christianity, as sisters and brothers in the two-thirds world have shown us parts of the gospel we in the past ignored.

As part of the World Methodist Council I have had my eyes opened time after time to how justice and evangelism go together. As the Spirit has moved in power and churches have doubled in just a few years, I have seen the Methodist and other churches at the forefront of demolishing apartheid in South Africa and attacking poverty in Rio.

Recently I was interviewing Clive Calver who is President of World Relief, an American organisation which works through the churches to help the poor. I asked him whether he missed his job as General Secretary of the Evangelical Alliance where he had done outstanding work. He told me story after story of people's lives being changed and the effect on him of seeing both injustice and hope. In the passion of his answer I was reminded of the passion of Jesus in caring for the poor.

What does God want for his people? Micah asks the same question. 'What does the Lord require of you? To act justly and to love mercy and to walk humbly with your God' (Micah 6:8). This is not just the legal following of the law, saying the right things, or being judgemental of others. It is goodness and loving consideration, in particular care for the weak.

Those who stress holiness, worship and the life of the Spirit need to hear this most of all. The prophet Isaiah speaks the word of the Lord who is appalled by the worship of people who do not care for justice, 'Stop doing wrong, learn to do the right! Seek justice, encourage the oppressed. Defend the cause of the fatherless, plead the case of the widow' (Is 1:17).

Who is the most holy person you know? Maybe a great evangelist or preacher. Maybe someone who prays a lot. Maybe someone who demonstrates many spiritual gifts. You would say that they knew the Lord well. But in Jeremiah a 'good' king is defined as 'He did what was right and just, so all went well. He defended the cause of the poor and needy . . . Is that not what it means to know me, declares the Lord' (Jer 22:15). God desires justice for all the world and God's people are to reflect God's own character. The theologian Tom Wright states, 'The church is to be not only an example of God's intended new humanity, but the means by which the eventual plan, including the establishment of worldwide justice is to be put into effect.'

So do we care for the poor and needy, not just in what we talk about but what we do? Every few years in the UK a group of media personalities sponsor Comic Relief, a fund-raising event for projects both in the UK and overseas. Many TV programmes are taken over by mad-cap sponsorship or other money-raising ideas. It was symbolic that one of the main religious programmes on the BBC during Comic Relief week had a major discussion on the ethics of fundraising – rather than actually doing any fundraising! It reminded me just how much the Church is like that, and how often I am too involved in talking about holiness rather than getting on and being holy.

When I came as a minister to Liverpool I came with a great agenda for change. By God's grace we have seen many of those changes happen. What I did not fully realise at the start was how much God wanted to change me. I felt the congregation needed to change, but God used the people to change me. My view of holiness had been about prayer, Bible knowledge and evangelism. Now, living in the one of the poorest cities in Europe, I still saw the importance of those things but I began to see other things too.

What about the man who lives down the street who needs help in claiming his benefit? What about the woman attacked by her husband? What if we employ staff at wages that are simply unjust for work? God was concerned about those things.

The congregation challenged me to think further afield. What about writing letters for Amnesty International? What could we do in the campaign for the cancellation of the unpayable debt of poorer countries? What about buying tea, coffee and other produce that has been fairly traded? These things are not side issues to the gospel or the life of holiness. To live a holy life is to pursue justice.

In C. S. Lewis' classic *The Screwtape Letters*, the devil advises a younger devil on how to corrupt the world. At one point he says, 'It is not necessary to make people wicked. Just make them indifferent. Don't worry about getting people to do bad things; just let them do nothing at all. Provide me with people who do not care.'

One night in a street in London a teenager called Stephen Lawrence was attacked by a gang of youths. He was attacked and killed simply because he was black. The subsequent public inquiry concluded the following police investigation was hampered by 'structural racism' and the whole attitude of British society needed to be changed. We cannot be indifferent to such issues. Our holiness should provoke us to get involved. Do we care to act? Whatever we think theologically about other faiths, we need to be at the forefront of the fight against racism. Whatever we think about the role of women in the church, we need to be at the forefront of the fight against sexism. Whatever we think about how the gospel relates to politics, we need to be at the forefront of the fight against poverty and for economic justice. For if we are not, then 'The time has come for judgement to begin with the household of God' (1 Peter 4:17).

Study and Action

One book to read: D. Evans and M. Fearon, *From Strangers to Neighbours* (Hodder Headline: London, 1998).

One outline for discussion:

1. Do you find the justice of God encouraging or challenging?
2. How can you promote God's concern for justice through your local fellowship?
3. What issues of justice are there in your local community?

4. What campaigns for justice in the world are you already involved in or could be involved in?

One question for yourself: Read Isaiah 1:17. What does it say to your life?

One action to take: Form a world justice group in your church. Meet to pray together and talk about what you can do. You only need to meet a couple of times a year to begin to make a difference.

14

WHOLESOME HOMES

Tinky Winky, Dipsy, La La and Po have caused a sensation in the UK. For the unenlightened they are not environmental campaigners or new kinds of cake, but characters in a children's television programme called *Teletubbies*. These coloured characters with television screens in their tummies and baby language for conversation provoked a national debate about the education of children. Some parents and educators complained that these odd characters are a bad influence for the development of children, although the children themselves love them.

The concern over *Teletubbies* went as quickly as it arose, but it highlights two issues in our society. One is the concern for what feels like an increasing sense of breakdown in our society and the tendency to blame someone else. Whenever the breakdown of relationships, lawlessness, the growth of drug abuse, or lower moral standards is mentioned then it is very easy to point the finger at government, the local authority, television, the Church or teachers. Christians can be especially outspoken in criticising others for lack of Christian standards.

The second issue is much more subtle. How do children learn and develop, especially in the area of morals? Governments, television and teachers often reply to criticism by stressing that the key influence is what happens in the home. In that they have the Bible on their side. For the Bible would say that the influence of *Teletubbies* is neither here nor there, but the influence of the home can both help and hinder holiness in the individual and the world.

I have lived in a number of different homes. First with my parents, then as a student in halls of residence, then as a single person, then as a married man and now in an extended family of my wife, children and students who live with us. In all of these situations, I find the following passage, though written in a very different context, says a number of challenging things:

> [13]So if you faithfully obey the commands I am giving you today – to love the Lord your God and to serve him with all your heart and with all your soul – [14]then I will send rain on your land in its season, both autumn and spring rains, so that you may gather in your grain, new wine and oil. [15]I will provide grass in the fields for your cattle, and you will eat and be satisfied.
>
> [16]Be careful, or you will be enticed to turn away and worship other gods and bow down to them. [17]Then the Lord's anger will burn against you, and he will shut the heavens so that it will not rain and the ground will yield no produce, and you will soon perish from the good land the Lord is giving you. [18]Fix these words of mine in your hearts and minds; tie them as symbols on your hands and bind them on your foreheads. [19]Teach them to your children, talking about them when you sit at home and when you walk along the road, when you lie down and when you get up. [20]Write them on the door-frames of your houses and on your gates, [21]so that your days and the days of your children may be many in the land that the Lord swore to give your ancestors, as many as the days that the heavens are above the earth.
>
> (Deuteronomy 11:13–21)

Deuteronomy is built on the key themes of the responsibility of the people of God to listen to, love, worship, serve and obey God (eg Deut 11:1). The motives for that obedience are God's love to them, the fact that he has already acted in history to save them, and that by following his plan then it will be good for them (Deut 11:1–17). It takes the form of a covenant between God and his people. God promises his unending love and grace, and the people need to respond with the obligations of grace.

The question arises as to how that obedience to God's way is maintained, with the many temptations of living in a land where others will try and lead you astray (v16). The solution is that God needs to be the focus of everything that goes on in life. One of the key verses in this passage is verse 18 where the writer says 'fix these words of mine in your hearts and minds'. These words are God's commands. Rather than simply leave them on tablets of stone, make them central to your life.

This poses the question, how do I make God's words central to my life? It is easy to be tempted to say that I must go to a good church where there are others who will both demonstrate and speak God's words. Or I must make sure that I receive regular good preaching and teaching from faithful women and men of God. Or I must make sure that I go to a place where I get good worship. As a parent of young children I also want to say that I need to find a good place for the children where they will be taught well about Jesus.

All of these things are important, but they have a practical difficulty and a danger. The difficulty is in finding a church where all these things are true! As a leader of a local church I am the first to see how far short we fall. I also see in the congregation some spiritual junkies who move from one church to another, trying desperately to find the perfect church. Nothing breaks my heart more than seeing people come to our church and then leaving. Sometimes the fault is ours but sometimes they are looking for a church which does not exist.

The danger is that in doing this we are shifting responsibility for our own learning and obedience, or that of our children, onto others. As I write this book we are planning to move house to another part of the country. This will involve us leaving a church where our children receive high quality Bible teaching and love. We know nothing of the church that we will attend in the future, but we do worry about whether there will be the same provision for the children. But in thinking that way we are shifting responsibility.

Deuteronomy is strong on the importance of public worship, but in this passage it balances it by saying that the key area is not the temple but the home. It is in the home that we learn basic principles of behaviour. It is where we are the most real and honest about ourselves rather than the public persona that we all project.

So what does it mean to have a holy home?

1. Holy homes are to be the place for signs and symbols

In order to fix God's words in their hearts and minds the writer suggests to the people that they 'tie them as symbols on your hands and bind them on your foreheads' (v18b). There is debate over whether this was taken literally but it gave rise to the practice of writing verses on small scrolls, placing them in little leather containers and binding them on the forehead and left arm (phylacteries). In addition, 'write them on the door-frames of your houses and on your gates' (v20). Once again this led to the practice of enclosing written passages in a small container and attaching them to the door-post of the house.

Why should such a practice be encouraged? It does seem an odd thing to do. However, symbols are both an aid to memory and a witness to others. The tying of a knot in a handkerchief is meant to remind you of something important. The writing on the door-posts no doubt recalled the Passover, when blood was put on the door frames of the Israelite slaves' houses as the first stage of God leading the people out of Egypt (Ex 12). But symbols also bring the private to the public. The ring I wear is not only a constant reminder for me of my wife's love, it is also a public sign of her love for me and my commitment to her. The symbols of Deuteronomy 11 are an encouragement to remember, but they are also about giving an awareness that God's love was constant and public.

What is the parallel for us? I remember seeing a house in the Channel Islands which was literally covered with biblical verses. Should that be the way for all Christians? If it was, we may have difficulty when it comes to selling our houses! I remember too a friend of mine who visited his grandparents who had a plaque on their living room wall with the words 'the eyes of the Lord are forever on you'. He said that it scared him enormously. He felt these eyes following him as in a horror movie. Of course, pictures, symbols and texts are helpful around the house. In my parents' house there is the verse, 'My God will supply all your needs according to his glorious riches in Christ Jesus' (Phil 4:19). During times of difficulty and uncertainty I would simply look at that verse and find God speaking to me.

Not only texts. As God has created this universe and given us the gift of creativity, there are many ways to symbolise God's love, both to help us remember and as a witness to others. As a travelling preacher I have the privilege of staying in many Christian homes. I have seen a lot of signs and symbols. Pictures of the wonders of creation from spiral galaxies to DNA speak of God's care and extravagance in creation. Paintings, prints and sculptures speak to people in different ways. Books and magazines, videos and music can all communicate the relevance and presence of God and give an atmosphere to a home.

As people visit our homes, we need to ask whether they encounter the holiness of God? Our homes are the places where we are most truly ourselves. Whether it is a room in a student hall of residence, a flat or a house, does it speak of the difference God makes to our lives?

Yet we have to be careful. It is very easy to descend into legalism, destroying the very thing it is meant to be about. In a passage we looked at earlier, Jesus criticises the teachers of the law and the Pharisees for such an error. 'Everything they do is done for men to see: They make their phylacteries wide and the tassels on their garments long'(Mt 23:5). Biblical texts or music will not in themselves move us to obedience. They may become a way for us to try and look good in front of others. Behind the symbols needs to be reality. The symbols should remind us of his love and his salvation, but do we demonstrate those things in our homes? We can have every biblical poster that has ever been made stuck to our walls, but do we show patience to flat-mates who drive us up those walls, kindness to parents or children, and generous hospitality to those outside of our homes? Are our homes places where we demonstrate self-giving love, forgiveness, truth and justice?

2. Holy homes are to be the place of important conversations

The writer of Deuteronomy wants us to weave faith into the tapestry of everyday life. So in terms of God's words, 'Teach them to your children, talking about them when you sit at home and when you walk along the road, when you lie down and when you get up' (v19).

This does not mean that we should always be discussing pre-destination over the washing-up or be constantly nagging those who are not Christians. It is about letting faith penetrate our conversations so that it is no longer private but public. It is about giving space to it in the normal run of the day.

We need to be ready to talk naturally and graciously about faith. Whether late at night or early in the morning. When watching the television, driving the car, eating lunch, or playing computer games, there might be times to talk about the faith. But in addition to that we need to make time and space to talk. I find the television soap, the football or the computer game has great value in unwinding and enjoyment, but I need to remember that time needs to be safeguarded for talk. As a leader of a large busy church I am often conscious that I speak about Jesus a lot to people but then view home as a retreat, giving less time to my wife and children in talking about the Christian faith than to others.

Of course not every conversation needs to explicitly name the name of Jesus. All ages need someone to show Christian love by simply listening. A conversation is never 'wasted' if it deepens a friendship, for friendship is the bridge that Jesus can use to walk into someone's life. The Christian faith is about the whole of life. Conversations of fun, creativity, politics, science and many other things can become places where relationships are strengthened and contexts where Jesus naturally comes in.

For those of us with children we cannot shirk our responsibility. The moral and religious education of children can be helped or hindered by government, teachers, the Church or television, but our children will learn the faith and model the faith from what they see in us. If we are parents, godparents, grandparents, aunts, uncles, nieces, nephews, brothers or sisters, neighbours or friends then what we do at home has immense significance. For those who live alone a home can be created where the love of God can be experienced. This does need hard work. Conversations about Christian faith do not always happen naturally. The people closest to you are often the most difficult to talk to about faith. But Christians of this generation need to recapture this vision for our homes. We have often separated faith into contexts outside of the home. Our picture of evangelism is that of big arenas and professional preachers. Our pictures of the passing down of the Christian faith are of theological colleges, books and full-time pastors.

Homes however are a strategic part of affecting wider society, not only in the education of our children. Under communist rule in Eastern Europe the Christian faith survived not primarily by church buildings or pastors, but often by the influence of grandparents who would teach the faith quietly and gently. The amazing growth of the Church there now is in large part due to that teaching.

The home is the most natural place for evangelism and learning. Here in Liverpool there are sections of the city which are totally alienated from the Christian Church. There are church buildings in the areas but they are 'peopled' by folk who faithfully travel in each week from a large distance away. The community itself cannot be reached through the buildings. It seems to me that we must sell the buildings and give that money to support Christians who will go, live and set up home in these communities. There in the day-by-day signs and symbols of Christian life, in the conversations Christ will be communicated.

Viscount Tonypandy commenting on British society said, 'Don't put the blame on teachers. If society has lost its way, it's because it has lost its faith . . . our faith decides our conduct and moral standards.' Why have we lost the faith? In large part because we as Christians have not lived it out in every part of our lives.

Study and action

One book to read: J. Drane, *Homes and Families* (Lion: Oxford, 1995).

One outline for discussion:
1. What do you find most difficult about life at home?
2. What is good about life at home?
3. How can your local fellowship support you better in your home life?
4. How can you use your home as a place for sharing Jesus?

One question for yourself: Is my conduct in my home less holy than in the church?

One action to take: Host a holy party – make it the best, celebrating the joy, love and acceptance of Jesus!

CONCLUSION

The young man who arrived as a new student at the University of Oxford was 'sick'with the desire to be holy. He was the son of an Anglican clergyman and he wanted to follow in his father's footsteps. He studied for ordination and was ordained a priest. He was by any standards obsessed with holiness. He wrote, 'I began to aim at and pray for inward holiness.' During his time at Oxford he tried to live such a life. He became leader of the 'Holy Club', a group of men who lived a life of strict discipline and met together regularly to check up on one another. Each morning and evening they spent an hour in private prayer, three times a day they recited a particular prayer, read the Bible frequently, noted signs of goodness and sin in coded diaries, meditated one hour a day, and fasted twice a week. They also attempted good works, by visiting prisoners and poor families, and beginning school classes for children.

You will quickly realise that he was not quite a typical student even if he did go to university in the 1720s. The student's name was John Wesley, and his group were given the name 'Methodists' because of their methodical pursuit of a holy life.

The trouble was that Wesley was pursuing it in the wrong way. In 1735 he went to Georgia as a missionary but the trip was one of failure, frustration and controversy. He lacked any inward peace. The more he strived to get inward peace through discipline, good works and trying to be holy, the more it seemed beyond him. During his trip to Georgia, however, Wesley had been impressed with the faith of a group of Christians called the Moravians. It seemed relevant to their everyday life and seemed to give them inner peace. On his return to England he talked more with them. He began to see that holiness is not achieved alone by human effort. He was right to see its importance, for 'without holiness no-one will see the Lord' (Heb 12:14). However, he did not fully recognise that holiness was about relationship with God. As the writer of the letter to the Hebrews points out, God works in us 'that we may share in his holiness' (Heb 12:10).

The turning point for Wesley came on 24 May 1738. At a meeting in Aldersgate Street, while listening to Luther's preface to his commentary on Paul's letter to the Romans, something happened. Wesley described it: 'I felt my heart strangely warmed. I felt I did trust in Christ, Christ alone for salvation; and an assurance was given me that he had taken away my sins, even mine, and saved me from the law of sin and death.' What actually happened is much debated. Some say it was conversion, some say baptism in the Spirit. Perhaps we will never fully know. What is clear is that Wesley experienced the love and life of God in a new way. He encountered the personal possibilities of grace and saw that holiness was the life of God in a person.

The effect was not a retreat back to the Holy Club, although prayer, Bible reading and fellowship remained vital to the development of this new life. Wesley understood God to be calling him to spread 'scriptural holiness over the land'. He saw that God's holiness had practical consequences. It was not simply individualistic, inward and insular. In 1739 he wrote: 'Holy solitaries is a phrase no more consistent with the gospel than holy adulterers. The gospel of Christ knows of no religion but social, no holiness but social holiness.'[1]

His holy life meant preaching in the fields rather than in the churches, travelling during his lifetime on horseback the equivalent distance to the moon, social concern such as homes for widows and orphans, free health clinics, help with food and clothing, the founding of schools, the support of new Christians through the organisation of societies and bands, books of hymns, Bible study notes, books of prayers, children's prayers and 400 books of adult Christian literature! One of his last letters was to William Wilberforce, encouraging the pursuit of the abolition of the slave trade.

With his brother Charles, John Wesley founded the Methodist Church which now has over 60 million members, but also had a profound effect on other churches and indeed the life of nations. Later in his life, in his catechism for the Methodist people, he wrote:

> What was the rise of methodism? In 1729 two young men, reading the Bible, saw that they could not be saved without holiness, followed after it, and incited others so to do. In 1737 they saw holiness comes by faith. They saw likewise, that men are justified before they are sanctified; but still holiness was their point. God then thrust them out, utterly against their will to raise a holy people.[2]

Wesley had to walk a tightrope. Often misunderstood and indeed persecuted by those in the churches for such things as outdoor preaching, he stayed true to the biblical faith and took seriously getting involved in the world.

We need to recapture today in our own generation the mission of spreading scriptural holiness. In the preceding chapters I have tried to illustrate what scriptural holiness is all about. Holiness is not about becoming so separated from the real world that you become a holy hermit. Holiness is about being really different so that you can make a real difference.

Where does the difference come from? It comes from a day-by-day relationship with God. It is no longer conforming to the pattern of this world but being transformed by the renewing of our minds (Rom 12:2). As we come to God time after time, repenting of what we have done wrong, receiving his forgiveness and asking for his guidance and power, so he will renew us and use us to make a difference.

J. I. Packer puts it in this way:

> Personal holiness is personal wholeness – the ongoing reintegration of our disintegrated and disordered personhood as we pursue our goal of single-minded Jesus-likeness; the increasing mastery of our life that comes as we learn to give it back to God and away to others; the deepening joy of finding worthwhileness in even the most tedious and mundane tasks when tackled for the glory of God and the good of other people; and the peace that pours from the discovery that, galling as failure in itself is, we can handle our failures – we can afford to fail, as some daringly put it – because all along we live precisely by being forgiven, and we are not required at any stage to live any other way.[3]

Holiness is never an end in itself. As John White puts it, 'To pursue holiness is to pursue God himself, to seek his face.'[4] John Wesley found that to be true. As God himself met with him, his life was transformed and he was 'thrust out' into the world. He was not the only Christian of past generations to encounter this. My prayer is that in this new generation, men and women will walk the tightrope and spread scriptural holiness. Yet, as always, this needs to start with me.

Notes

1. *Works of John Wesley* (London, 1872), Vol VI, p.145.
2. *Works of John Wesley* (London, 1872), Vol VIII, p.300.
3. J. I. Packer, *A Passion for Holiness* (Crossway Books; Nottingham, 1992), p.93.
4. John White, *Holiness* (Eagle: Guildford, 1996), p.7.

DO YOU NEED A SPEAKER?

Many Monarch authors, including the author of this book, are willing to come and speak to groups of all sizes. To obtain a list of authors and topics, please write to: Monarch Books, Concorde House, Grenville Place, Mill Hill, London NW7 3SA.

The Joy of Fearing God

Fearing God seems hardly an occasion for joy. Yet the fear of the Lord is actually the key that opens the door to a life of true knowledge, wisdom, blessing – and above all, joy.

Join Jerry Bridges as he unveils the awesome greatness of God: His incredible holiness, unsearchable wisdom, and especially His inspiring love. You will gain a deeper understanding of who God is that will draw you into a truly biblical – and surprisingly delightful – fear of God.

'Reading Jerry Bridges is like eavesdropping on an angel enraptured by adoration. He understands the fear of God as an awe-filled reverence before the divine majesty. This book will expand the mind and loose the soul to soar on high.' – R C SPROUL

The Joy of Fearing God
Jerry Bridges
ISBN 1 85424 453 1

Available from your local Christian Bookshop.
In case of difficulty contact Monarch Books, Angus Hudson Ltd,
Concorde House, Grenville Place, Mill Hill, London NW7 3SA

MONARCH
BOOKS